Beautiful Foods

Caroline Bimbo Afolalu 2015 All Rights Reserved

The rights of Caroline Bimbo Afolalu to be identified as the author of this work have been asserted in accordance with the Copyright, Designs and Patents Act 1988

All rights reserved. No Part may be reproduced, adapted, stored in a retrieval system or transmitted by any means, electronic, mechanical, photocopying, or otherwise without the prior written permission of the author or publisher.

Spiderwize
Remus House
Coltsfoot Drive
Woodston
Peterborough
PE2 9BF

www.spiderwize.com

The views expressed in this work are solely those of the author and do not necessarily reflect the views of the publisher, and the publisher hereby disclaims any responsibility for them.

Beautiful Foods: The Art of African Catering

Featuring the very best of Nigerian recipes
with
expert tips for a perfect wedding
By
Caroline Bimbo Afolalu

First Published in Great Britain in 2014
1st edition
By
Whitstone Books

www.beautifulfoods.co.uk

Welcome

Caroline Bimbo Afolalu

Dedication

This book is dedicated to my husband Tunde Afolalu. Over the years I have found in you the rare and unique virtue of patience.

...my wonderful children Bisi, Pelumi and Ife Afolalu

Acknowledgements

- I give glory to God, the author and finisher of our faith, first, for I am fearfully and wonderfully made and for perfecting all that concerns me.

- I thank my parents late Mr & Mrs Omolase who were retired school teachers in Nigeria, for putting me through great education and seeing to it that I graduated first with second class upper class BA (Hons) English Language 1990 class of University of Ibadan Nigeria, and also with LLB (Hons) 1997 class of Metropolitan University London.

- I thank my husband who has been my rock and support and my wonderful children who have been great blessings in my life. You rock my world, thank you.

- My thanks to our mentor and accountant Michael Jegede and Tony Goldstein, our business advisor, for making my dream a reality and making sure I always think big and strategically.

- Many thanks to all my family, friends, customers and staff at Beautiful Foods Ltd, my social network friends and my church family.

- Finally to my dear friends Shola Akere, Omolara Ololade and Omolade Fafowora, your love and support mean the world to me. Thank you for all your hard work and contribution in making sure this book is a success.

Thank You

Contents

Introduction	6
Health & Safety	7
Sourcing Ingredients	10
Street & Finger Snacks	12
Soup & Starters	41
Main Meals	46
Stews	66
Accompaniments	84
Salads	84
Poultry	87
Beef	90
Fish	91
Snail	92
Heavy Meals	93
Desserts	99
Fruit Salads	99
Biscuits	103
Cakes	105
Misc	118
Fresh Fruits & Nuts	122
Drinks	127
How To	130
Home Cooking Menu Ideas	139
Healthy Eating	144
How to plan Weddings and Parties	149
Wedding Menu Ideas	157
Theme and Venue for Parties	163
Picnic Menu Ideas	164
Photo gallery	165
Glossary	170
Index	172

Introduction

Growing up as a Yoruba girl in Nigeria, West Africa, I have always been fascinated with how simple food ingredients could be put together to make beautiful and delicious meals. Being the last girl of six children, I spent the most time with my mother cooking West African dishes for the family.

After getting married and migrating to the UK, my first mission was to conquer sourcing West African Ingredients and cooking beautiful meals for my family and friends. I love to cook and enjoy the presentation side of food; I see food as an art.

After completing my law degree, I had a desire to mentor and teach both adult and young people the art of West African cooking, so I enrolled at South Bank University Bakery School where I graduated with food technology after two years of intense studies.

It is my aim to open the door of Beautiful Foods' recipes to the world by introducing you to the wealth of West African cooking. My great expectation is that this recipe book will help my readers, both Africans at home and in the Diaspora, and people from other cultures to understand the richness of West African cuisine, party etiquette and Nigerian culture whilst enjoying the beauty and taste of food from our great continent - Africa.

Health & Safety

I learnt quickly, whilst studying food technology at South Bank University Bakery College, the importance of food safety during cooking and food manufacturing.

Food hygiene is essential in ensuring food does not become contaminated by bacteria which can cause food poisoning leading to illness. There is a good practice to follow in cooking and production of safe food. These principles are also underpinned by food safety laws.

Legislation (Food safety Act 1990)
- Food must be of the nature, substance or quality demanded.
- Food must not present any risk to health, and must be fit for human consumption.

Good Personal Hygiene

Hands must be washed especially:

When entering the kitchen or food factory
- After using the toilet
- After smoking
- After handling refuse
- After cleaning
- After eating or drinking
- After touching your face, nose or hair
- After sneezing or coughing

Health & Safety

Nails

Nails should be kept clean and short with no nail polish.

Cuts

Cuts, boils and skin infection should be covered with coloured waterproof plaster.

Illness

People suffering from Illness such as diarrhoea or any other illness that may be infectious must not handle food for communal eating.

Hair

Hair should be kept tied back for home cooking and covered for commercial cooking.

Jewellery

Rings (except a plain wedding band), watches and necklaces must be removed before cooking

Make Up

Strong perfume and aftershave have strong smells that can be transferred to food. These should be avoided when preparing meals.

Protective Clothing

Outdoor clothing may carry germs. A clean apron should be worn when preparing meals.

Cleaning

A high standard of hygiene and housekeeping should be maintained at all times. Clean all work surfaces and equipment before and during cooking using a clean cloth and safe cleaning chemicals.

Health & Safety

Cross Contamination

- Avoid cross contamination whilst storing food in the fridge, keep raw meat or poultry covered and place at the bottom of the fridge to avoid blood or uncooked juices dripping onto other food.
- Keep raw food away from ready to eat food, store fruit and vegetables away from meat and poultry.

Temperature Control

- Follow the instructions on storage and cooking temperatures on ingredient labels.
- Keep the fridge temperature at 5-8 degrees centigrade.
- Keep the freezer temperature at -18 degrees centigrade.
- Cook food thoroughly and where possible use a thermometer to probe food. The temperature should be above 70 degrees centigrade.
- Cut poultry and meat during cooking to check there is no blood in the centre.
- Buy ingredients from reputable suppliers.

"As of Asher his food shall be rich, and he will yield royal dainties."

Genesis 49:2

Sourcing Ingredients

It is necessary to select food ingredients suitable for cooking West African food. The first challenge to great cooking is knowing where to buy the necessary ingredients.

Key West African Ingredients

Whilst most ingredients used in African cooking are the same as the rest of the world, for example Africans use the same flour, sugar, salt, milk, vegetable oil, butter, eggs, rice, potatoes, poultry, meat, fish, salads and vegetables such as chillies, tomatoes and onions, there are certain food unique to the continent of Africa. Below is a list of a few of such food ingredients.

- Yam
- Plantain
- Egusi (melon seeds)
- Isapa (hibiscus flower)
- Brown beans
- Gari (processed cassava)
- Pounded yam flour (a mixture of flours)
- Amala (plantain or yam flour)
- Palm oil
- Suya spice

The above list of ingredients are now readily available in Europe and the rest of the world. They can be obtained from the following places:

Street Markets

All ingredients used in this book can be purchased from local street markets in Nigeria and most West African countries.

Grocery shops

Most ingredients used in the key recipes can be purchased from Afro Caribbean grocers in street markets in England, Europe, Canada and USA.

Supermarkets

The major supermarkets in England now stock Afro Caribbean ingredients in their ethnic sections.

Online shops

Some online shops do sell ingredients for African cooking. These can be found through internet search engines.

Street & Finger Snacks

Some food items are known as street snacks in Nigeria, West Africa. These food items are readily available from open market and roadside stalls.

Roasted Corn (Barbecue Corn)

Ingredients

2 pieces of sweet corn on the cob

Preparation Method

1. Remove the outer leaves from the corn.
2. Place the corn onto a hot charcoal or electric barbecue. (An oven may be used).
3. Cook every side of the corn for about 20 minutes or until the corn is golden brown.
4. Remove the roasted corn and serve on a plate.

Boiled Corn (Corn on the Cob)

Ingredients

2 fresh corn on the cob

1 tsp salt (optional)

1 litre water (for boiling)

Preparation Method

1. Place the corn and the salt into a saucepan of water.
2. Boil for 35 minutes or until the corn is soft.
3. Drain the boiled corn from the water.
4. Cool and serve.

Roasted Plantain (Barbecue Plantain)

Ingredients

2 plantain (ripe or unripe)

Preparation Method

1. Peel the plantain, place it on a hot charcoal or electric barbecue. (An oven may be used.)
2. Cook the plantain, turning it around until all sides are golden brown.
3. Remove the roasted plantain and serve on a plate.

Notes

Popularly wrapped in paper and eaten with roasted groundnut.

Boiled Plantain

Ingredients

2 plantains (ripe or green)

1 tsp salt (optional)

1 litre water (for boiling)

Preparation Method

1. Cut the plantains in two, slit the skin with a knife.
2. Place the plantain with the skin on or peeled into a saucepan of water.
3. Add the salt and boil for 30 minutes or until the plantain is soft.
4. Serve.

Street & Finger Snacks

Roasted Yam (Barbecue Yam)

Ingredients

½ yam tuber

Preparation Method

1. Wash and dry the yam, cut into large pieces (do not peel).
2. Place the yam slices on a hot charcoal or electric barbecue. (An oven may be used.)
3. Cook the yam for about 50 minutes, turning it around until all sides are dark brown.
4. Remove the roasted yam, peel the skin and serve on a plate.

Notes

Roasted yam could be eaten with butter or palm oil and fresh chilli sauce.

Suya (Beef Kebab)

Ingredients

500g boneless meat (lamb or beef)

2 tbsp suya pepper seasoning

1 tsp chilli pepper

½ onion

1 fresh tomato

2 tablespoon vegetable oil

Preparation Method

1. Wash and slice the meat thinly, about 4mm thickness.
2. Sprinkle the meat slices with suya and chilli pepper seasoning.
3. Rub the seasoned meat slices with vegetable oil using a soft brush.
4. Push the meat slices onto a wooden skewer.
5. Place the meat slices in a bowl, cover and place in the fridge for at least 1 hour to marinate.
6. Place the meat slices onto a hot charcoal or electric barbecue. (A grill may be used).
7. Cook the meat slices for about 40 minutes or until meat is tender.
8. Remove from the stick and serve with onion slices and fresh tomato slices.

Suya (Beef Kebab)

Street & Finger Snacks

Assorted Suya

Ingredients

1kg boneless meat (beef tripe & beef)

2 tbsp suya pepper seasoning

1 tbsp hot chilli powder

1 tbsp all purpose seasoning

1 tsp dried thyme

1 tsp hot curry powder

½ onion & garlic

1 Maggi cube

1 tsp salt

Vegetable oil (for frying)

2ltr water

Preparation Method

1. Wash and dice the beef and beef tripe.
2. Sprinkle the diced meat with all the seasoning except the suya and chilli pepper.
3. Place the meat slices in a bowl, cover and place in the fridge for at least 1 hour to marinate. This step is optional, you may skip and continue to boiling step.
4. Place the meat in a saucepan, add the water and boil for about 60 minutes or until the meat is soft and tender.
5. Fry in a hot oil at 180 degrees for 6 minutes or until the centre of the meat is dry of water.
6. Drain off excess oil on a paper tissue and cool.
7. Sprinkle with suya seasoning and chilli pepper.
8. Ready to serve.

Assorted Suya

Street & Finger Snacks

Dry Roasted Peanut

Ingredients

200g raw peanuts

1g salt

20ml cold water

Preparation Method

1. Place the peanuts in a baking tray.
2. Add the salt and water and mix in.
3. Place in pre heated oven and roast at 150 degrees for 15 minutes.
4. Cool and serve with skin or skin removed.

Notes

Roasted peanuts can also be stir-fried in a wok over low heat.

Roasted Peanuts & Popcorn

Ingredients

200g raw peanuts

100g dried corn grains

1 tbsp honey

Preparation Method

1. Place the peanuts in a wok over low heat (or roast in oven for 15 minutes at 150 degrees).
2. Stir with a wooden spoon until the peanuts are brown.
3. Remove the peanuts from the pan and cook the corn until all the grain starts to pop.

4. Add a teaspoon of honey to the corn and stir.
5. Serve the roasted peanuts with the popcorn.

Boiled Groundnut

Ingredients

200g monkey nuts (groundnuts in shells)

1ltr water (for boiling)

Preparation Method
1. Place the groundnuts into a saucepan of water.
2. Boil for 35 minutes or until the groundnuts are soft.
3. Drain boiled groundnut from the water.
4. Cool and serve.

Aadun (Ground Roasted Corn Snack)

Ingredients

500g dried corn grains

2 tbsp palm oil

½ tsp salt

Preparation Method
1. Place the dried corn grains into a thick bottomed pan.
2. Stir fry over a low heat until they're brown.
3. Cool the cooked corn grains, grind in a mill into a fine flour.
4. Add the palm oil and salt, wrap in cling film or banana leaves
5. Ready to serve.

Street & Finger Snacks

Akara (Beans Cake)

Ingredients

200g beans (Nigerian Beans)

½ chilli or cayenne pepper

½ onion

½ tsp salt

½ cup cold water (to blend beans)

Vegetable oil (for frying)

Preparation Method

1. Soak the beans in cold water for 1-2 hours.
2. Rub the soaked beans with both hands until all the skin comes off the beans.
3. Wash the skin off the beans until it is white.
4. Blend the beans, onion and pepper with little water into a smooth paste, the consistency must be thick, not like batter, otherwise the akara will not form into balls in the oil.
5. Pour the blended beans into a bowl and mix with a spoon.
6. Add the salt and mix with a spoon.
7. Heat the vegetable oil in a shallow pan to about 160 degrees.
8. Scoop a tablespoon full of beans paste and drop into the hot oil.
9. Fry on a medium heat, turning over until both sides are golden brown.
10. Check the centre of the akara with a fork to ensure the centre is cooked.
11. Drain the excess oil off on a paper towel.
12. Serve with custard or ogi (pap) at breakfast.

Notes

This delicacy has become a money making food item. Local women fry them by road sides or in street markets.

Osu, a village in Osun state of Nigeria, is most popular for this trade.

Young city people eat this delicacy with African loaf bread.

Ojojo (Water Yam Cakes)

Ingredients

1 water yam

1 small onion (diced)

1 fresh chilli pepper (diced)

1 tsp salt

Vegetable oil (for frying)

Preparation Method
1. Wash, peel and grate the water yam into a bowl.
2. Add the salt, chilli pepper and diced onion.
3. Heat the oil in a frying pan and drop in tiny balls of grated yam.
4. Fry at 160 degrees for about 10 minutes or until golden brown.
5. Drain off excess oil on a paper tissue and serve.

Street & Finger Snacks

Plantain Crisps

Ingredients

1 plantain (green or mid ripe)

½ tsp salt

Vegetable oil (for frying)

Preparation Method

1. Pre heat the fryer to 180 degrees.
2. Place the plantain on a chopping board.
3. Cut the tip and the tail off using a knife.
4. Slit the plantain across the middle from top to bottom.
5. Remove the skin from the plantain, using a knife.
6. Cut the plantain into 2mm or 3mm round discs.
7. Sprinkle with salt and fry at 180 degrees for 3-5 minutes or until all the sides are golden brown.
8. Drain off the oil on a paper towel.
9. Ready to serve

Notes

The secret to achieving the crunchiness in plantain crisps is in the thickness, anything above 3mm will give you a soft plantain more like ordinary fried plantain. You may want to use a slicer to achieve a nice and consistent cut.

Flavours

1 tsp of chilli pepper may be added for peppered flavour.

Plantain Crisps

Street & Finger Snacks

Chin Chin

This is a delicious West African snack loved by most Africans. It is popularly served at Christmas, parties and festive times. I remember rolling and cutting chin chin as a child with other children at Christmas time. It is great to have in the house for snacking.

Ingredients

200g plain flour

60g granulated sugar

25g margarine or butter

½ tsp nutmeg

5ml vanilla flavouring

20ml milk (fresh or skimmed powder)

1 egg

40ml water

Vegetable oil (for frying)

Preparation Method

1. Mix the flour, sugar, margarine and nutmeg in a bowl.
2. Add water, milk, egg and vanilla and mix to a dough.
3. Dust a table with flour and roll the dough to ¼ inch thickness using a rolling pin.
4. Cut the dough into small cubes or strips using a sharp knife.
5. Fry the strips in a hot oil at 180 degrees for 8 minutes or until golden brown.
6. Drain off the excess oil on a paper towel, cool and serve.

Notes

For soft textured Chin Chin, add extra butter, eggs or baking powder.

For coconut flavour, add 50g designated coconut to the flour and 10ml coconut essence.

For chilli flavour reduce sugar to half and add 1 tablespoon chilli pepper to the flour.

Chin Chin

Street & Finger Snacks

Barbecue Chicken

Ingredients

8 drumsticks or other chicken parts

1 tbsp barbecue chicken seasoning

1 tbsp vegetable oil

1 tsp chilli pepper

1 tsp thyme

Preparation Method

1. Rub the chicken seasoning, thyme and chilli pepper onto chicken parts.
2. Add a tablespoon of vegetable oil and mix.
3. Leave the seasoned chicken in a fridge for at least 1 hour to marinate (optional).
4. Cook in an oven, grill or charcoal barbecue for 45 minutes.
5. Cut the centre of the chicken to check that it is thoroughly cooked without blood.
6. Serve with rice or potato dishes.

Scotch Egg

Ingredients

6 eggs

300g sausage meat

50g wheat flour (for dusting hand)

1 tsp chilli powder

100g bread crumbs

1 egg (whisked with a little water for egg wash)

500ml water (for boiling the eggs)

Preparation Method

1. Boil the eggs in a saucepan of water for 10 minutes.
2. Cool the eggs in a bowl of cold water.
3. Peel the boiled eggs and set aside.
4. Mix the sausage meat and chilli powder.
5. Dust your hands with the flour.
6. Scoop an egg-size lump of sausage meat and roll into a ball.
7. Flatten the sausage meatballs and place an egg in the centre.
8. Wrap the flattened sausage meat around the boiled egg to form a ball.
9. Dip into the beaten egg wash.
10. Dip into the breadcrumbs until it's well coated.
11. Repeat the process until all the eggs are done.
12. Fry the scotch eggs in a deep fryer at 160 degrees for 6-8 minutes.
13. Drain off excess oil on a paper tissue and serve.

Street & Finger Snacks

Scotch egg

Fried Yam Chips

Ingredients

½ tuber of yam

Vegetable oil (for frying)

1 tsp salt

Preparation Method

1. Peel the skin of the yam, cut into strips and place into salt water.
2. Drain the yam strips from the water.
3. Heat oil in a pan and fry the yam at medium heat until golden brown.
4. Drain off the excess oil on a paper towel.
5. Serve with sauce.

Assorted Stick Meat

Ingredients

500g diced beef

150g diced beef tripe

100g diced chicken gizzard

½ onion

1 tsp thyme

1 tsp salt

1 Maggi cube

1 red & green paprika pepper

2 tbsp vegetable oil

2 tbsp all-purpose seasoning (suya pepper may be used)

2ltr water

Street & Finger Snacks

Preparation Method

1. Season and cook the meat pieces in a saucepan of water, salt and Maggi cube for 1 hour.
2. Drain the cooked meat from the water.
3. Cool the meat pieces and set aside on a plate.
4. Dice the pepper and onions and set aside.
5. Arrange the meat pieces, diced onions and peppers onto a wooden barbecue stick.
6. Arrange the stick meat on a baking tray, sprinkle with suya seasoning and vegetable oil.
7. Place the stick meat into a hot oven or a grill and cook at 160 degrees for 10 minutes or deep fry.
8. Serve on a bed of lettuce leaves, great as a starter dish at parties.

Meat Pie (Minced Beef & Potato Patty)

Ingredients

Pastry

500g plain flour

200g margarine

150ml water

½ tsp baking powder

½ tsp salt

1 egg (whisked with a little water for egg wash)

Filling

500g minced beef (freshly ground beef)
2 potatoes (diced)
2 carrots (diced) optional
½ tsp chilli pepper
½ tsp salt
1 Maggi cube
½ tsp (all purpose) seasoning
½ dried thyme (fresh herb may be used)
30g flour (plain or corn flour mixed with a little water)
100ml cold water

Preparation Method

A. Preparing the Pastry

1. Place flour, margarine, salt and baking powder in a mixing bowl.
2. Mix the flour mixture into crumby texture (about 5 minutes).
3. Add cold water and mix to a firm dough.
4. Wrap in cling film and rest in a fridge for 30 minutes.

B. Preparing the Filling

1. Stir fry the minced beef in a saucepan for 5 minutes.
2. Keep stirring to avoid it burning.
3. Add the diced potatoes, carrot, chilli pepper, salt, Maggi, thyme and seasoning.
4. Add the water and simmer for 15 minutes.
5. Add the flour mixed with a little water to thicken.
6. Pour onto a shallow tray or a bowl placed in shallow cold water for faster cooling, it should be cooled to 37 degrees within 90 minutes to avoid bacteria and food poisoning.
7. Once it is cooled, set aside.

Street & Finger Snacks

C. Making the Pie

1. Roll out the pastry to ¼ inch thickness about (2-3mm).
2. Cut into round shapes with a large round pastry cutter about 5 inches wide.
3. Place the filling in the centre of the pastry.
4. Brush one edge of pastry with the beaten egg wash using a pastry brush.
5. Fold over the other edge to cover the filling.
6. Seal with the finger tips or a fork (plastic patty maker may be used).
7. Place onto a paper lined tray.
8. Brush the top of pies with the beaten egg wash using a pastry brush.
9. Bake at 180 degrees in a pre-heated oven for 30 minutes or until golden brown.
10. Ready to serve.

Meat Pie (minced beef & potato patty)

Sausage Roll

Ingredients
500g plain flour
200g margarine
150ml water
½ tsp baking powder
½ tsp salt
1 egg (beaten with a little water for egg wash)

Filling
500g sausage meat
1 tsp thyme
½ tsp chilli pepper

Preparation Method

A. Making the Pastry
1. Place flour, margarine, salt and baking powder in a mixing bowl.
2. Mix the flour mixture into crumby texture (about 5 minutes).
3. Add cold water and mix to a firm dough.
4. Wrap in cling film and rest in a fridge for 30 minutes.

B. Preparing the Filling
Mix the sausage meat with the chilli pepper and thyme, set aside for later.

C. Making the Pie
1. Roll the short crust pastry on a floured board to ¼ inch thick rectangle.
2. Cut into 4 x 4 inch strips.
3. Place the seasoned sausage meat in strips onto the centre of the rolled pastry.

Street & Finger Snacks

4. Brush one edge of the pastry with beaten egg wash.
5. Fold over the other edge of the pastry strip to cover the sausage meat.
6. Fold over once again and place onto paper lined trays.
7. Brush the top with the beaten egg wash using a pastry brush.
8. Cut the top with a knife to create vents for the steam.
9. Bake in a pre-heated oven at 180 degrees for 30 minutes.

Sausage roll

Vegetable pie

Ingredients

Pastry

500g plain flour

200g margarine

150ml water

½ tsp baking powder

½ tsp salt

1 egg (beaten with a little water for egg wash)

Filling

80g mixed vegetables

70g mixed peppers

½ tsp salt

½ tsp chilli pepper

½ tsp seasoning (any of your choice)

2 potatoes (diced)

1 cup of water

2 tbsp cream cheese (optional)

Preparation Method

A. Making the Pastry

1. Place flour, margarine, salt and baking powder in a mixing bowl.
2. Mix the flour mixture into crumby texture (about 5 minutes).
3. Add cold water and mix to a firm dough.
4. Wrap in cling film and rest in a fridge for 30 minutes.

Street & Finger Snacks

B. Preparing the Filling
1. Place the potatoes in a saucepan with a little water.
2. Cook for 10 minutes.
3. Add the peppers, mixed vegetables, salt, seasoning and chilli.
4. Cook for 5 minutes.
5. Add the cream cheese.
6. Cool and set aside.

C. Making the Pie
1. Roll the pastry on a floured board to ¼ inch thick rectangle.
2. Cut into 4 x 4 inch strips.
3. Place the seasoned vegetable filling onto the centre of the rolled pastry.
4. Brush one edge of the pastry with the beaten egg wash using a pastry brush.
5. Fold over the other edge of the pastry strip to cover the filling.
6. Fold over once again and place onto paper lined trays.
7. Brush the top with the beaten egg wash using a pastry brush.
8. Cut the top with a knife to create vents for the steam.
9. Bake in a pre-heated oven at 180 degrees for 30 minutes.
10. Ready to serve.

Fish Pie/Roll

Ingredients

Pastry

500g plain flour

200g margarine

150ml water

½ teaspoon baking powder

½ teaspoon salt

1 egg (beaten with a little water for egg wash)

Filling

500g fish fillet

1 chilli pepper

½ tsp salt

½ tsp black pepper

½ tsp fish seasoning

100ml water

1 tbsp corn flour or plain flour (mixed with water to thicken)

Preparation Method

A. Making the Pastry
1. Place flour, margarine, salt and baking powder in a mixing bowl.
2. Mix flour mixture into crumby texture (about 5 minutes).
3. Add cold water and mix to a firm dough.
4. Wrap in cling film and rest in a fridge for 30 minutes.

Street & Finger Snacks

B. Preparing the Filling

1. Poach fish in a saucepan with water, pepper, salt and seasoning.
2. Add the corn flour to thicken.
3. Cool and set aside in a bowl.

C. Making the Pie

1. Roll out the pastry to ¼ inch thickness on a board or floured table.
2. Cut the rolled pastry into 3 x 4 inch strips or any size of your choice using a knife or cutter.
3. Place the filling in the centre of pastry using a spoon.
4. Brush one edge of the pastry with the beaten egg wash using a pastry brush.
5. Fold over the other edge of the pastry to cover the filling.
6. Press firmly and fold over once again to a sausage shape.
7. Place onto a paper lined tray.
8. Cut the top of the fish pie with a knife to create a vent for the steam.
9. Brush the top with the beaten egg wash using a pastry brush for a gloss finish.
10. Bake in a pre-heated oven for 30 minutes at 180 degrees.
11. Ready to serve.

Buns

Ingredients

250g self-raising flour

60g granulated sugar

15g margarine

½ tsp nutmeg

½ tsp vanilla

20ml fresh milk (or 20g skimmed powder)

200ml water (may vary depending of the flour texture)

Vegetable oil (for frying)

Preparation Method

1. Mix the flour and margarine well together in a bowl.
2. Add the nutmeg, sugar and mix in with a spoon or electric mixer.
3. Add the vanilla, milk and water and mix until a soft paste is formed.
4. Scoop a little of the paste with your hand, make into a small ball shape.
5. Drop into hot oil and fry on medium heat of about 160 degrees.
6. Test the centre with a fork to ensure it is thoroughly cooked.
7. Drain off the excess oil on a paper towel and serve.

Notes:

The consistency of the mix should be between a soft dough and a thick paste.

Street & Finger Snacks

Puff Puff (African Doughnut)

Ingredients

250g self-raising flour

60g granulated sugar

½ tsp nutmeg

7g dried yeast

½ tsp salt

½ tsp vanilla

2 tbsp milk or powdered milk (optional)

250ml warm water (water quantity may vary depending on the flour texture)

Vegetable oil (for frying)

Preparation Method

1. Mix all the dry ingredients in a bowl.
2. Add the warm water, vanilla and milk.
3. Mix with a wooden spoon until a smooth, thick paste is formed.
4. Cover the mix and place in a warm place to ferment for about 1 hour.
5. Heat the vegetable oil in a saucepan or deep fryer.
6. Scoop a small ball shape with a spoon or wet hand and drop into the oil.
7. Fry on a medium heat about 160 degrees until golden brown.
8. Test the centre of the puff puff with a fork to ensure it is cooked.
9. Drain off excess oil on a paper tissue and serve.

Soup & Starters

Notes:

The consistency of the mix should between a soft paste and a thick batter.

Pepper Soup (Assorted Goat Meat)

Ingredients

300g diced goat meat

100g diced tripe

100g diced cow foot

1 onion

½ tsp chilli pepper or fresh chilli

½ tsp fresh ground ginger

1 tbsp pepper soup spice

1 tsp salt

1tsp thyme

1tsp curry

Fresh mint (any herb could be used)

1 clove garlic

2ltr water

Preparation Method

1. Place all the ingredients except the chilli and the herbs in a saucepan.
2. Add water and cook meat for 1 hour or until the meat is soft and tender.
3. Add the herbs and chilli pepper to taste.
4. Serve with bread roll and butter.

Soup & Starters

Meat pepper soup

Isi Ewu (Igbo Traditional Goat Head Pepper Soup)

Ingredients

1 goat head (chopped into bite sizes)

1 onion

1 tsp chilli pepper

1 tbsp pepper soup spice

1 tsp salt

1tsp thyme

1tsp curry

2 Maggi cubes

Ukazi leaves (any herb could be used)

Ehuru seeds

Preparation Method

1. Place all the ingredients except the chilli, palm oil and the herbs in a saucepan.
2. Add some cold water and cook the goat meat for 1 hour or till tender.
3. Add the palm oil, herbs and chilli pepper to taste.
4. Ready to serve.

Soup & Starters

Fish pepper soup

Ingredients

1 Fresh fish (smoked catfish can be used)

1 onion

½ tsp chilli pepper

½ tsp ground fresh ginger

1tsp pepper soup spice

½ tsp salt

½ tsp thyme

½ tsp curry

Fresh mint

½ garlic clove

1ltr water

Preparation Method

1. Clean and wash the fish.
2. Add the water and boil for 10 minutes.
3. Place all the ingredients except the chilli and the herbs in a saucepan.
4. Add a little water and cook fish for 10 minutes.
5. Add the herb and chilli pepper to taste.
6. Serve with bread roll.

This is great for parties or when feeling poorly.

Fish pepper spup

Main Meals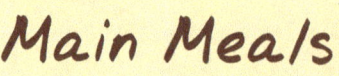

Grilled Fish & Lemon Wedges

Ingredients

1 fresh or frozen fish

1 lemon

¼ lettuce

1 tsp fish seasoning

1 tsp salt

1 tsp chilli pepper

2 tbsp vegetable oil

Preparation Method

1. Clean, wash and place the fish onto a foil paper lined tray.
2. Add the salt, pepper and seasoning to the fish.
3. Add the vegetable oil and rub into the seasoned fish.
4. Place in a hot oven or a grill and cook for 20 minutes at 180 degrees.
5. Serve with lemon wedges on a bed of lettuce.
6. This makes great accompaniment with chips, fried plantain or rice dishes.

Jollof Rice

Ingredients

800g brown easy cook rice

400g tinned tomato (fresh may be used)

1 red paprika pepper

1 scotch bonnet or chilli pepper

1 onion

1tbs salt to taste

2 Knor cubes or Maggi cubes

1 tbsp all purpose seasoning

2 tbsp tomato puree

60ml vegetable oil

1 tbsp dried thyme

2 bay leaves (fresh or dried)

1200ml water

Preparation Method

1. Blend the tomatoes, peppers, onions until smooth.
2. Heat the vegetable oil in a saucepan.
3. Add the blended tomatoes and peppers and tomato puree.
4. Add all the seasoning, knor or Maggi cubes and salt.
5. Cook the sauce for 5 minutes.
6. Wash and drain the rice, add the rice into the sauce.
7. Add some of the water and lower the heat.
8. Simmer for 35-45 minutes, adding the remaining of the water until rice is soft and dry.

Notes:
Jollof rice is the most popular meal used at parties and festive period.

Main Meals

Jollof Rice served with Plantain & Salad

Fried rice served with chicken and salad

Fried rice

Ingredients

500g brown easy cook or basmati rice

150g mixed vegetable

50g mixed peppers

100g cooked prawns (optional)

2 tbsp vegetable oil

1tsp salt

1 tsp all-purpose seasoning

1 tsp thyme

1 twin Knor cube or 2 Maggi cubes

1ltr water

Preparation Method
1. Wash the brown rice and drain out the water.
2. Heat the vegetable oil in a saucepan.
3. Add the rice and all the seasoning and stir fry lightly for 5 minutes.
4. Lower the heat and add the water. Cook for 40 minutes.
5. Add the mixed vegetables, peppers and the prawns.
6. Steam the fried rice for 5 minutes or until the rice is soft, adding a little water whenever dry.
7. Serve with fried meat, mixed salad or fried plantain.

Main Meals

Fried rice served with chicken and salad

Boiled rice (white rice) served with stew

Boiled rice (White Rice)

Ingredients

500g brown rice

1tsp salt

1ltr cold water

Preparation Method
1. Wash the rice and place in a saucepan of water.
2. Add the salt and boil for 35 minutes or until rice is soft.
3. Drain the water out of the rice or lower the heat to dry out.
4. Serve with stew.

Main Meals

Boiled Yam

Ingredients

½ a tuber of white yam

1 tsp salt

1ltr water

Preparation Method

1. Peel and slice yam, wash and place into a saucepan.
2. Add the water and salt.
3. Boil the yam for 30 minutes or until the yam is soft.
4. Drain off the water and serve with stew or fried egg.

Yam Porridge

Ingredients

½ a tuber of white yam

200ml parboiled stew or freshly blended tomatoes and peppers

1 tsp Salt

1 Maggi cube

1tsp aroma

500ml water

30ml vegetable oil

Preparation Method

1. Peel and dice the yam.
2. Wash and place the diced yam in a saucepan of water.
3. Add a little water, enough to just cover the yam.
4. Add the salt and cook for 20 minutes on low heat.
5. Add the seasoning and par boiled stew.
6. Stir and add more stew until the yam is reddish in colour.
7. Add the vegetable oil and simmer for 5 minutes.
8. Serve with fried stew

Notes:

You may add a little sugar if yam is new harvest.

Main Meals

Yam Porridge

Beans and Sweetcorn

Ingredients

500g brown or white black eyed beans

400g tinned sweetcorn

1 onion

1tsp salt

6 tbsp par boiled stew or freshly blended tomatoes and pepper.

1 tbsp palm oil (vegetable oil may be used)

2 ltr water

Preparation Method

1. Wash and place the beans and diced onions in a saucepan of water.
2. Cook the beans for 50 minutes.
3. Add the sweetcorn and salt, cook for 10 minutes.
4. Add the stew and palm oil, simmer for 10 minutes.
5. Ready to serve.

Main Meals

Beans and Boiled Yam

Ingredients

500g brown Nigerian beans

2 slices of peeled yam (diced)

1 onion

1 tsp salt

6 tbsp par boiled stew

1 tbsp palm oil

2 ltr water

Preparation Method

1. Wash and place the beans and diced onions in a saucepan of water.
2. Cook the beans for 40 minutes.
3. Add the diced yam and salt, cook for 20 minutes.
4. Add the stew and palm oil, simmer for 10 minutes.

Beans

Ingredients

500g brown beans

1 tsp salt

6 tbsp par boiled stew (freshly blended tomatoes and pepper can be used)

1 onion

6 tbsp palm oil

2 ltr water for cooking

Preparation Method

1. Boil the beans and the diced onions in a saucepan of water for 1 hour.
2. Add the salt and par boiled stew, simmer for 10 minutes.
3. Add the palm oil and simmer the beans until it is thick.
4. Serve with fried plantain, loaf bread or drinking gari.

Beans served with plantain

Main Meals

Beans (Ewa Agayin)

Ingredients

500g brown beans

1 tsp salt

2 ltr water

Preparation Method

1. Cook the beans and salt in a saucepan of water for 1 hour.
2. Lower the heat and simmer for 10 minutes.
3. Serve with fried stew, plantain or loaf bread.

Rice and Beans

Ingredients

350g brown rice

150g brown beans or black eyed beans

1 tsp salt

2 ltr water

Preparation Method

1. Cook the beans in a saucepan of water for 40 minutes.
2. Add the rice, salt and cook for 30 minutes.
3. Drain off the water and serve with stew.

Notes:

Beans and rice can be cooked separately and served together in a plate.

Coconut Rice

Ingredients

500g brown rice

1 coconut (tinned coconut milk may be used)

1 tsp salt

1ltr water

Preparation Method
1. Grate the coconut into a bowl of water.
2. Drain the coconut water into a saucepan.
3. Add washed rice, salt and cook for 30 minutes.
4. Serve with stew.

Ofada Rice (Nigerian Local Rice)

Ingredients

500g Ofada rice

1 tsp salt

1ltr water

Preparation Method
1. Ensure the rice is clean.
2. Wash and add into a saucepan of boiling water.
3. Add salt and cook for 30 minutes.
4. Drain and serve with stew.

Main Meals

Fried Plantain

Ingredients

1 ripe plantain

½ tsp salt (optional)

Vegetable oil (for frying)

Preparation Method

1. Pre heat the fryer to 180 degrees.
2. Place the plantain on a chopping board.
3. Cut the tip and the tail off using a knife.
4. Slit the plantain across the middle from top to bottom.
5. Remove the skin from the plantain.
6. Cut the plantain diagonally into ½ inch slices.
7. Sprinkle with salt (optional).
8. Fry the plantain at 180 degrees for about 5 minutes or until all the sides are golden brown.
9. Drain off the oil on a paper towel.
10. Ready to serve.

Note:

The difference between plantain crisps and fried plantain is the thickness. Fried plantain is cut into about ½ an inch diagonal slices or cubes while plantain crisps are cut into about ¼ of an inch round discs or diagonal slices.

Boiled Sweet Potatoes

Ingredients

2 sweet potatoes

½ tsp salt

500ml water

Preparation Method

1. Peel and cut the potatoes into big chunks.
2. Boil the potatoes in a saucepan of water and salt.
3. Cook for 20 minutes or until tender.
4. Serve with stew.

Notes:

Sweet potato can be fried to make chips or crisps.

Gari (Roasted Grated Cassava)

Ingredients

½ cup gari

1 tbsp sugar (optional or to taste)

300ml water

Preparation Method

1. Place the gari into a bowl or glass of cold water.
2. Ready to serve.

Notes

Gari is a great accompaniment with beans, roasted ground nuts and moimoi.

Main Meals

Pap /Ogi (African Custard)

Ingredients

2 tbsp fermented corn dough

1 tbsp sugar (optional)

400ml water

100ml milk (optional)

Preparation Method

1. Boil the water in a saucepan.
2. Mix the corn dough with cold water to become liquid.
3. Pour the mix into the boiling water, stir and simmer for 2 minutes.
4. Serve with the milk and sugar.

Notes:

This is best served at breakfast with Akara or Moimoi.

Moimoi

Ingredients

300g Nigerian beans

1 red paprika pepper

1 scotch bonnet pepper

1 onion

2 boiled eggs (optional)

Crayfish or flaked fish (optional)

3 tbsp vegetable oil

1 tsp salt

Leaves or foil tins (for wrapping during cooking)

2 ltr water

Preparation Method
1. Soak the beans in water for about 1-2 hours.
2. Rub with the palm of your hands until skins come off.
3. Wash off the skin from the beans until they are completely white.
4. Blend the peeled beans with a little water.
5. Add the peppers and onion and blend into a thick batter.
6. Add the vegetable oil, salt and flaked fish or crayfish.
7. Fill folded plantain leaves or foil tins until half full.
8. Add sliced egg to each portion and cover or seal.
9. Place a wire rack at the bottom of a saucepan to prevent water getting into the Moimoi.
10. Add a little water to cover the base of the pan.
11. Place the wrapped moimoi in the pan.
12. Add water frequently to prevent the moimoi from burning.
13. Steam moimoi for 60 minutes.
14. Press the top to check if moimoi is ready. Cooked moimoi should be firm to touch.
15. Serve with eko, hot pap, custard or gari.

Main Meals

Cocoyam

Ingredients

2 pieces of cocoyam

500ml water

Preparation Method
1. Peel and wash the cocoyam, cut into big slices.
2. Boil the cocoyam in a saucepan of water until soft.
3. Drain and serve with stew.

Notes:

Cocoyam may be used as a substitute for yam.

Milk Bread

Ingredients

1kg wheat bread flour

20g salt

20g sugar

5g nutmeg

40g yeast

30g margarine

50g skimmed powder

300ml water (warm)

Preparation Method

1. Sieve the flour into a bowl.
2. Add the skimmed milk, salt, sugar, yeast, nutmeg and margarine.
3. Add the water and mix into a dough.
4. Knead with the knuckle on a floured table till smooth.
5. Cover and leave in a warm place to ferment for 1 hour.
6. Once dough is doubled up in size, place on floured board and knead.
7. Grease baking pans with margarine.
8. Cut the dough into small sizes and smoothen with hand.
9. Place into the baking pan and leave in warm place to rise.
10. Bake the dough at 220 degrees for 30 minutes.
11. Serve the bread with beans, butter or egg stew.

Stews

Stew with Assorted Meat

This is a stable stew for every African home.

Ingredients

800g tinned tomatoes (or fresh)

1 onion

2 chilli peppers or scotch bonnet peppers

1 red paprika pepper

6 tbsp vegetable oil

1kg assorted cooked meat or fish

2 Maggi cubes

1 tsp salt

200ml water

Preparation Method

1. Blend the tomatoes, peppers and onion in a blender.
2. Heat the vegetable oil in a saucepan.
3. Pour in the blended tomatoes and peppers.
4. Add the salt, Maggi or any seasoning of your choice.
5. Boil the stew for 1 hour, adding the water as required.
6. Add the cooked meat or fish.
7. Simmer for 5-10 minutes.
8. Remove from the heat and cool.

Stew with Assorted Meat

Stews

Egg Stew

Ingredients

4 fresh eggs

2 fresh tomatoes

½ onion

1 Maggi cube

¼ tsp salt

½ chilli or fresh pepper

1 tbsp vegetable oil

Preparation Method

1. Roughly blend the tomatoes, pepper and onion in a blender.
2. Heat the vegetable oil in a saucepan.
3. Add the blended tomatoes and peppers.
4. Simmer for 10 minutes to make a stew.
5. Add salt and Maggi cube or any seasoning of your choice.
6. Whisk the egg and add into the stew.
7. Simmer for 5 minutes.
8. Serve with boiled yam, loaf bread or plantain.

Notes:

Sardine can be added to make sardine and egg stew.

Vegetable Stew (Efo Riro)

Ingredients

500g chopped spinach (frozen or fresh)

400g tinned or fresh tomatoes

1 onion

2 chillis or scotch bonnet peppers

1 red paprika pepper

2 Maggi cubes

1 tsp salt

4 tbsp vegetable oil (or palm oil)

200g assorted fried meat

100g dried fish or crayfish (optional)

Preparation Method

1. Roughly blend the tomatoes, peppers and onion in a blender.
2. Heat the oil in a saucepan and add the blended tomatoes and pepper.
3. Add the salt, Maggi and seasonings.
4. Simmer for 10 minutes.
5. Add the fried meat and dried fish, cook for 10 minutes.
6. Add the spinach and cook for 5 minutes.
7. Serve with heavy meal or keep refrigerated for weekly use.

Notes:

Delicious served with pounded yam.

Stews

Egusi with Spinach

Ingredients

500g ground egusi (melon seed)

400g tomatoes

2 chillis or scotch bonnet peppers

1 onion

1 red paprika pepper

500g spinach (chopped)

1tsp salt

2 Maggi cubes

6 tbsp vegetable oil or palm oil

200g fried meat

100g dried fish and crayfish (optional)

Preparation Method

1. Blend the tomatoes, onion and peppers in a blender (frozen par boiled stew may be used).
2. Heat the oil in a saucepan and add the blended tomatoes.
3. Add the salt, Maggi and seasonings.
4. Simmer for 15 minutes.
5. Add the fried meat and dried fish.
6. Mix the egusi with a little water and mix into a paste (freshly ground whole egusi can be used).
7. Drop a spoonful of egusi paste into the stew, do not stir.
8. Simmer for 15 minutes, stir with a wooden spoon.
9. Add the spinach, stir and cook for 5 minutes.
10. Serve with heavy meals or keep refrigerated for later use.

Egusi and Isapa with Assorted Meat

Ingredients

500g ground egusi (melon seed)

400g tomatoes

2 chilli or scotch bonnet peppers

1 onion

1 red paprika pepper

250g dried isapa (hibiscus flower)

1 tsp salt

2 Maggi cubes

6 tbsp vegetable oil or palm oil

200g fried meat

100g dried fish and crayfish (optional)

Preparation Method

A. Processing the isapa
1. Soak the dried isapa in water for 4 hours or overnight.

B. Preparing the soup
1. Wash the soaked isapa and cut into small pieces using the finger, set aside.
2. Blend the tomatoes, onion and peppers in a blender (frozen par boiled stew may be used).
3. Heat the oil in a saucepan and add the blended tomatoes.
4. Add the salt, Maggi and seasonings.
5. Simmer for 15 minutes.
6. Add the fried meat and dried fish.

Stews

7. Mix the egusi with a little water and mix into a paste (freshly ground whole egusi can be used).
8. Drop spoonful of egusi paste into the stew, do not stir.
9. Simmer for 15 minutes, stir with a wooden spoon.
10. Add the isapa, stir and cook for 10 minutes.
11. Serve with heavy meals e.g. traditional pounded yam or keep refrigerated for later use.

Okra (plain)

Ingredients

100g okra

1 tsp salt

1 Maggi cube

20g iru /locust beans (optional)

50ml water

Preparation Method

1. Grate the okra and place in a saucepan of water.
2. Add the Maggi, salt and iru (locust beans).
3. Boil the okra for 8-10 minutes.
4. Serve with stew as accompaniment with heavy meals or keep refrigerated for later use.

Okra in stew

Ingredients

100g okra
1 fresh tomato
½ chilli pepper
1 Maggi cube
½ tsp salt
20g iru /locust beans (optional)
1 tbsp palm oil
100g assorted meat
100g dried fish or crayfish (optional)
2 tbsp water

Preparation Method

1. Blend the tomatoes and pepper and place in a saucepan.
2. Add the salt, Maggi and iru and boil for 10 minutes.
3. Add the fried meat or fish.
4. Whisk the okra with tablespoon of water and pour in.
5. Add the palm oil and simmer for 5 minutes.
6. Serve with heavy meals or keep refrigerated for weekly use.

Stews

Ogbono

Ingredients

200g ground ogbono

1 fresh tomato

1 chilli or scotch bonnet pepper

½ tsp salt

2 Maggi cubes

20g iru/locust beans (optional)

1 tbsp palm oil

150g assorted fried meat or fish

100g dried fish or crayfish (optional)

100ml water

Preparation Method

1. Blend the tomato and pepper in a blender.
2. Place into a saucepan and boil for 10 minutes.
3. Mix the ground ogbono powder with the water and add in.
4. Add the salt, Maggi and iru locust beans.
5. Simmer for 15 minutes.
6. Add the meat or fish and simmer for 5 minutes.
7. Serve with heavy meals or keep refrigerated for later use.

Garden Egg

Ingredients

2 large aubergine or 6 small garden eggs

1 fresh tomato

1 chilli pepper

1 onion

4 tbsp palm oil (vegetable oil may be used)

½ tsp salt

Preparation Method

1. Boil the garden egg in a saucepan of water until it is soft roughly about 10-15 minutes.
2. Cool the boiled garden egg and remove the skin (optional).
3. Mash the garden egg with a fork and set aside.
4. Roughly blend or chop up onions, tomato and pepper.
5. Heat the oil in a saucepan.
6. Add in blended or chopped onion, tomato and pepper.
7. Add the salt and simmer for 10 minutes.
8. Add the mashed garden egg into the stew and simmer for 5 minutes.
9. Serve with boiled yam or boiled plantain.

Stews

Ayamase Stew

Ingredients

6 green paprika pepper

2 green chilli pepper

30g iru /locust beans (ground)

30g ground crayfish

6 tbsp palm oil

3 onions

1 tsp salt

2 Maggi cubes

200g fried meat (bite sizes)

Preparation Method

1. Blend the peppers and onions in a blender.
2. Heat the palm oil in a saucepan until it is pale in colour.

    (Open kitchen windows, the process may smoke and can cause fire if left unattended, must not be left unattended)
3. Cool the oil and add the blended peppers and onions and simmer for 1 hour.
4. Add the salt, Maggi cube, iru, ground crayfish and meat pieces.
5. Simmer for 10 minutes.
6. Serve with plain rice.

Beans Stew

Ingredients

2 red paprika pepper

2 fresh chilli pepper

30g ground crayfish

4 tbsp palm oil (bleached)

1 onion

1 tsp salt

1 Maggi cube

Preparation Method

1. Blend the peppers and onions in a food processor.
2. Heat the bleached palm oil in a saucepan.
3. Add the blended pepper and onions and simmer for 30 minutes.
4. Add the salt, Maggi cube, ground crayfish and simmer for 30 minutes.
5. Serve with plain beans or yam porridge.

Stews

Pumpkin Stew

Ingredients

1 pumpkin

½ tsp salt

400g tinned tomato or fresh tomatoes

1 onion

4 tbsp palm oil

1 chilli pepper

1ltr water

Preparation Method

1. Slice the pumpkin into big chunks.
2. Remove the seeds, wash the pumpkin.
3. Place into saucepan of water, boil the pumpkin until it is soft.
4. Remove the skin and mash the pumpkin.
5. Heat palm oil in a saucepan.
6. Add the chopped or roughly blended tomatoes, onions and chilli.
7. Add the salt and seasoning.
8. Cook the sauce for 20 minutes, add the mashed pumpkin.
9. Simmer for 5 minutes.
10. Serve with boiled yam or plantain.

Uha soup

Ingredients

500g cooked assorted meat

200g dried stock fish (or smoked fish and crayfish)

500g uha leaves (fresh or dried)

2 tbsp palm oil

2 fresh chilli pepper

1 paprika pepper

1 onion

2 Maggi cubes

2 cocoyam (boiled and mashed)

1tbsp iru (locust beans)

Preparation Method
1. Soak the dried stock fish in water for 1 hour.
2. Boil in a saucepan of water until the fish is soft and tender.
3. Clean the boiled fish, break into small pieces with the fingers and set aside.
4. Blend the peppers and onions, pour into a saucepan and cook for 20 minutes.
5. Add the fish, cooked meat and crayfish.
6. Add the Maggi cubes, salt, palm oil and iru.
7. Boil the cocoyam, mash and drop into the soup in tiny balls to thicken.
8. Remove the uha leaves from its stems with the fingers, wash and add into the soup.
9. Simmer for 10 minutes and serve with heavy meal.

Stews

Edikang Ikong

Ingredients

500g cooked assorted meat

200g dried stock fish (or smoked fish and crayfish)

500g fresh pumpkin leaves

500g fresh water leaves

4 tbsp palm oil

2 fresh chilli pepper

1 paprika pepper

1 onion

2 Maggi cubes

100g periwinkle

Preparation Method

1. Soak the dried stock fish in water for 1 hour.
2. Boil in a saucepan of water until the fish is tender.
3. Clean the boiled fish, break into small pieces with the fingers and set aside.
4. Blend the peppers and onions, pour into a saucepan and cook for 20 minutes.
5. Add the fish, cooked meat and crayfish.
6. Add the Maggi cubes, salt, periwinkle and the palm oil.
7. Remove the leaves from the stems with fingers and wash.
8. Cut with the leaves with the fingers and add into the soup.
9. Simmer for 5 minutes and serve with heavy meal.

Bitter leaf soup

Ingredients

500g cooked assorted meat

200g dried stock fish (or smoked fish and crayfish)

500g dried bitter leaves

2 tbsp palm oil

2 fresh chilli pepper

1 paprika pepper

1 onion

2 Maggi cubes

2 cocoyam (boiled and mashed)

1tbp iru /locust beans

Preparation Method

1. Soak the dried stock fish in water for 1 hour.
2. Boil the soaked fish in a saucepan of water until the fish is tender.
3. Clean the boiled fish, break into small pieces with the fingers and set aside.
4. Soak the dried bitter leaves in a bowl of water.
5. Blend the peppers and onions, pour into a saucepan.
6. Cook for 20 minutes and add the dried fish, cooked meat and crayfish.
7. Add the Maggi cubes, salt, palm oil and iru.
8. Boil the cocoyam, mash and drop the cocoyam into the soup in tiny balls to thicken.
9. Remove the bitter leaves from water, squeeze out excess water and add the bitter leaves into the soup.
10. Simmer for 5 minutes and serve with heavy meal.

Stews

Banga

Ingredients

400g tinned banga (palm fruit pulp)

500g assorted cooked meat

1 smoked fish

50g crayfish

1 chilli pepper

1 tsp salt

2 Maggi cubes

50g scent leaves

Preparation Method

1. Pour the banga in a saucepan, and cook for 20 minutes.
2. Add the cooked meat and washed smoked fish.
3. Add the salt, Maggi cube, chilli pepper and the crayfish.
4. Simmer until a thick sauce is formed.
5. Add the scent leaves and cook for 5 minutes.

Ewedu (Jute or Marlow leaves)

Ingredients

100g ewedu leaves

1 tbsp. iru (optional)

½ tsp salt

1 Maggi cube

Potash (pinch)

100ml water

Preparation Method

1. Remove the ewedu leaves from the stem by hand.
2. Wash and blend roughly in a blender.
3. Place in saucepan of water.
4. Add the iru, a pinch of potash, salt and Maggi cube.
5. Boil the ewedu for 10 minutes.
6. Serve with heavy meals.

Accompaniments

Tomato and Lettuce Salad

Ingredients

4 fresh tomatoes

1 iceberg lettuce

1 tbsp salad cream (optional)

Preparation Method

1. Wash the tomatoes and lettuce, dry with paper towel.
2. Place the lettuce and tomatoes on a chopping board and cut to bite sizes.
3. Arrange the salad in a bowl.
4. Serve with salad cream.

Coleslaw

Ingredients

12 carrots

1 white cabbage

4 tbsp mayonnaise

Preparation Method

1. Wash the vegetables and dry with a paper towel.
2. Grate the carrot and shred the cabbage into a bowl.
3. Add the mayonnaise and mix well together.
4. Chill and serve as an accompaniment.

Salad

Accompaniments

Mixed Vegetable Salad

Ingredients

1 iceberg lettuce

2 carrots

1 cucumber

1 cabbage

2 tomatoes

400g tinned sweetcorn

2 tbsp salad cream (optional)

Preparation Method

1. Wash and dry all the vegetables.
2. Chop or slice all vegetable except tomatoes on a board.
3. Arrange the salad in a bowl or plate.
4. Drain the water from the sweetcorn and add.
5. Cut tomatoes into four and remove the seeds.
6. Dice the tomatoes and add to the salad.
7. Serve with salad cream.

Notes:

Cooked diced yam, potatoes, flaked fish, boiled egg or baked beans can be added.

Poultry

Spicy Gizzard in Pepper Garnishing

Ingredients

500g gizzard (chicken or turkey)

1tbsp chicken seasoning

½ tsp thyme

½ tsp curry

½ tsp salt

1 paprika pepper

1 onion

4 tbsp par boiled stew or blended tomato and pepper

2 tbsp vegetable oil

1 Maggi cube

2ltr water

Preparation Method

1. Wash the gizzard and place in saucepan of water.
2. Boil the gizzard with seasoning for 30 minutes and fry for 5 minutes at 160 degrees.
3. Heat the vegetable oil in a saucepan.
4. Add the sliced peppers and onions and stir fry for 2 minutes.
5. Add the blended tomatoes or parboiled stew.
6. Add the salt, Maggi and seasoning of your choice, cook for 10 minutes.
7. Add fried gizzard and simmer for 3 minutes.
8. Serve as accompaniment.

Poultry

Fried Chicken in Pepper Garnishing

Ingredients

1kg chicken thigh and leg (whole chicken or parts can be used)

1tsp salt

1tsp all-purpose seasoning

2 Maggi cubes

1 onion

1 paprika pepper

4 tbsp par boiled stew

2 tbsp vegetable oil

2ltr water

Preparation Method

1. Cut the chicken into big chunks (ask your butcher to cut them for you).
2. Place the chicken chunks in a saucepan of water.
3. Add the salt, Maggi and seasoning.
4. Cook for 1 hour or until tender.
5. Drain the chicken and fry in hot oil.
6. Slice the onions, paprika pepper and fry for 2 minutes.
7. Add the par boiled stew or freshly blended tomato and pepper.
8. Cook for 10 minutes and add in the fried chicken.
9. Stir and serve as accompaniment.

Fried Chicken & Beef in Pepper Garnishing

Beef

Fried Beef in Pepper Garnishing

Ingredients

1kg beef (any meat can be used)

½ tsp salt

½ tsp thyme

½ tsp curry

2 Maggi cubes

1 onion

1 paprika pepper

3 tbsp par boiled stew

2 tbsp vegetable oil

2ltr water

Preparation Method

1. Cut the beef into big chunks, you may ask your butcher to cut them for you.
2. Place the beef into a saucepan of water.
3. Add the salt, Maggi and seasoning.
4. Cook for 1 hour or until tender.
5. Drain the meat and fry in hot oil for about 5 minutes at 160 degrees.
6. Heat the vegetable oil in a saucepan.
7. Slice the onions, paprika pepper and stir fry for 2 minutes.
8. Add par boiled stew or freshly blended tomato and pepper.
9. Cook for 5 minutes and add in the fried meat.
10. Stir and serve as accompaniment.

Fish

Fried Fish in Pepper Garnishing

Ingredients

1 fish
½ tsp salt
½ fish seasoning
1 Maggi cube
1 onion
1 paprika pepper
4 tbsp par boiled stew
2 tbsp vegetable oil

Preparation Method

1. Clean and cut the fish into big chunks.
2. Add the salt and fish seasoning.
3. Deep fry for 10 minutes at 160 degrees, gently turning as fish can be fragile and break easily.
4. Heat the vegetable oil in a saucepan.
5. Slice onions, paprika pepper and stir fry for 2 minutes.
6. Add the par boiled stew or freshly blended tomato and pepper.
7. Add the Maggi and stir.
8. Cook for 10 minutes and add the fried fish or alternatively to avoid the fish breaking, you may arrange the fried fish in a serving dish and pour the sauce over the fish.
9. Serve as accompaniment.

Snail

Snail in Pepper Garnishing

Ingredients

2 pieces of snail

½ tsp salt

2 Maggi cubes

2 tbsp parboiled stew

½ paprika pepper (diced/sliced)

½ onion (diced)

1 tsp seasoning

1 tbsp vegetable oil

1 lime or lemon (for washing the snail)

1 alum (for washing the snail)

1 tbsp salt (for washing the snail)

1ltr water

Preparation Method

1. Remove the snail from its shell.
2. Wash the snail with the salt, lemon and alum to remove the slimy feel.
3. Rinse thoroughly with water until it is sharp to touch.
4. Cut the snail into small slices.
5. Boil in saucepan of water with salt, onion, one Maggi cube and seasoning.
6. Fry the snail for 5 minutes at about 160 degrees.
7. Stir fry the paprika peppers, onions and stew.
8. Add the other Maggi cube and the fried snail and stir.
9. Ready to serve.

Heavy Meals

Traditional Pounded Yam

Ingredients

1 tuber of yam

2ltr water

Preparation Method

1. Peel the yam, slice into chunky pieces.
2. Place into saucepan of water, boil for 30 minutes or until soft (check with a fork).
3. Place a few yam pieces in a wooden mortar and pound the yam with a pestle until it forms a marsh, avoid lumps.
4. Mix with hot water, gently pound and mix into a soft and soft dough.
5. Serve with vegetable stew.

Pounded Yam served with vegetable soup & assorted meat

Heavy Meals

Eba

Ingredients

200g gari

500ml water

Preparation Method

1. Boil the water in a kettle or a saucepan.
2. Pour the hot water in a bowl.
3. Add the gari into the boiled hot water.
4. Ensure the water covers the gari.
5. Cover and leave for 2 minutes.
6. Mix with a wooden spoon into a soft dough, avoid lumps.
7. Scoop into a plate or wrap in cling film or plastic bag
8. Serve with vegetable stew

Notes:

You may use more water for softer dough or less water for firmer/hard dough.

Heavy Meals

Amala

Ingredients

200g amala flour
700ml water

Preparation Method

1. Boil the water.
2. Pour 500ml of the boiled hot water into a saucepan.
3. Add the amala flour, stirring with a wooden spoon.
4. Mix into a smooth dough with a wooden spoon, avoid lumps.
5. Add the remaining hot water, cover and steam for 5 minutes.
6. Mix to a dough and serve with vegetable stew.

Ground Rice

Ingredients

200g ground rice flour
700 ml water

Preparation Method

1. Boil the water.
2. Pour 500ml of the boiled hot water into a saucepan.
3. Add the ground rice flour, stirring with a wooden spoon.
4. Mix into a smooth dough with a wooden spoon, avoid lumps.
5. Add the remaining hot water, cover and steam for 5 minutes.
6. Mix to a firm dough.
7. Serve with vegetable stew.

Pounded Yam (flour mix)

Ingredients

200g pounded yam flour

700ml water

Preparation Method

1. Boil 700ml water.
2. Pour 500ml of the boiled hot water into a saucepan.
3. Add the pounded yam flour, stirring with a wooden spoon.
4. Mix into a smooth dough using a wooden spoon, avoid lumps.
5. Add a little hot water, cover and steam for 5 minutes.
6. Mix to a firm dough.
7. Serve with vegetable stew.

Fufu

Ingredients

200g fufu flour

700 ml water

Preparation Method

1. Boil the water.
2. Pour 500ml of the boiled hot water into a saucepan.
3. Add fufu flour.
4. Mix into a dough until it is smooth, avoid lumps.
5. Add the remaining hot water, cover and steam for 5minutes.
6. Mix to a firm dough.
7. Serve with vegetable stew.

Heavy Meals

Semovita

Ingredients

200g semovita flour

700 ml water

Preparation Method
1. Boil the water.
2. Pour 500ml of the boiled hot water into a saucepan.
3. Add the semovita flour, stirring with a wooden spoon.
4. Mix into a dough or till smooth, avoid lumps.
5. Add the remaining hot water, cover and steam for 5 minutes.
6. Mix to a firm dough and serve with vegetable stew.

Fruit Salads

Tropical Fruit Salad

Ingredients

1 ripe pawpaw

1 ripe pineapple

1 mango

2 oranges

1 water melon

Preparation Method

1. Remove all the seeds and cut into cubes or bite sizes.
2. Place in a bowl and add the juice from the oranges.

Fruit Salad

Ingredients

1 kiwi

1 bunch of red grapes

1 apple

2 strawberries

10 blueberries

Preparation Method

1. Wash all the fruits, slice kiwi and apples into bite sizes.
2. Place in a dessert bowl.
3. Chill and serve

Fruit Salad

Fruit Skewer

Fruit Salads

Fruit Skewer

Ingredients

1 kiwi

2 blueberries

1 large apple

2 strawberries

50g plain chocolate (melted for dipping)

2 wooden skewers

Preparation Method

1. Wash all the fruits, cut the apples and kiwi into slices or cubes.
2. Pass the fruits through the wooden skewers.
3. Ready to serve.

Butter Biscuits

Biscuits

Butter Biscuits

Ingredients

250g plain flour

150g butter

150g caster sugar

1 egg

Preparation Method

1. Pre heat oven to 180 degrees.
2. Mix the butter into the flour and sugar.
3. Add the egg and mix into a dough.
4. Roll out the dough to about 5mm.
5. Cut with biscuit cutter or a knife into your desired shapes.
6. Place onto greased baking tray and bake at 180 degrees for 10 minutes.
7. Cool and serve.

Biscuits

Chocolate Chip Cookies

Ingredients

100g margarine

50g brown sugar

50ml egg (1 egg whisked)

5ml vanilla essence

150g self raising flour

Pinch of salt

5g ground cinnamon

175g plain chocolate chips

50g walnut

Preparation method

1. Pre heat oven to 180 degrees.
2. Mix margarine and sugar in a bowl until fluffy.
3. Add the egg and vanilla essence and mix in.
4. Add the flour, salt and cinnamon and mix in.
5. Add the plain chocolate and walnut and mix in.
6. Place teaspoon full of the dough onto baking trays (allow 2 inches apart)
7. Bake in pre heated oven at 180 degrees for 15 -20 minutes.
8. Cool and serve.

Cakes

Madeira cake

Ingredients

300g self-raising flour

150g margarine

150g caster sugar

150g egg (whisked)

50ml milk

1 tbsp vanilla

1 tsp nutmeg

Preparation Method

1. Preheat oven to 180 degrees
2. Mix the sugar and margarine with a spoon or a mixer for 5 minutes.
3. Add the whisked egg, vanilla and milk.
4. Add the flour and nutmeg.
5. Mix into a smooth batter for about 5 minutes.
6. Grease baking tin with some margarine using a pastry brush. Dust the greased tins with flour to take off excess fat.
7. Pour the cake batter into the greased baking tin.
8. Bake in pre heated oven at 180 degrees for 45 minutes.
9. Test the centre with a dry knife, if the knife comes out dry, the cake is ready.
10. Cool and serve or decorate.

Cakes

Victoria Sponge Cake
Ingredients

100g self-raising flour

100g margarine

100g caster sugar

100g egg (whisked)

25ml milk

1 tsp nutmeg

1 tsp vanilla

Preparation Method

1. Pre heat oven to 180 degrees
2. Cream the margarine and sugar in a bowl, until it is fluffy, using a wooden spoon or an electric mixer.
3. Add in the whisked egg gradually, add a little flour if the mix curdles.
4. Add the flour and nutmeg.
5. Add the milk and vanilla.
6. Mix to a smooth paste for about 5 minutes.
7. Grease a baking tin with some margarine using a pastry brush.
8. Dust the greased tin with some flour to remove excess fat.
9. Pour the cake batter into the greased baking tin.
10. Bake in a pre-heated oven at 180 degrees for 30 minutes.
11. Test the centre with a dry knife.
12. Cool and serve or decorate.

Cakes

Genoese Cake

Ingredients

150g self-raising flour

150g margarine

150g caster sugar

150g egg (whisked)

1 tbsp vanilla essence

Whipped cream (filling & topping)

Preparation Method

1. Pre heat oven to 180 degrees
2. Whisk the egg and sugar in a bowl, using a wooden spoon or an electric mixer.
3. Melt the margarine and add into the whisked egg/sugar mix.
4. Add the vanilla essence and mix in.
5. Add in the flour and mix for about 5 minutes.
6. Grease two baking tins with some margarine using a pastry brush.
7. Dust the greased tins with some flour to remove excess fat.
8. Divide the batter into the two greased tins.
9. Bake in the pre-heated oven at 180 degrees for 30 minutes.
10. Cool and sandwich with whipped cream.

Cakes

Banana Sponge Cake

Ingredients

150g self-raising flour

150g margarine

150g caster sugar

150g egg (whisked)

2 fresh bananas (mashed)

1 tablespoon vanilla essence

Whipped cream (filling)

Preparation Method

1. Pre heat oven to 180 degrees.
2. Cream the margarine and sugar in a bowl, using a wooden spoon or an electric mixer.
3. Add the whisked eggs and mix in the mashed bananas.
4. Add in the flour and mix into a smooth batter.
5. Grease two baking tins with some margarine using a pastry brush.
6. Dust the greased tins with some flour to remove excess fat.
7. Divide the batter into the two greased tins.
8. Bake in a pre-heated oven at 180 degrees for 25 minutes.
9. Cool and sandwich with whipped cream.

Cakes

Banana Walnut & Lemon Cake

Ingredients

250g self-raising flour

115g margarine

200g caster sugar

150g egg (whisked)

100ml milk

75g chopped walnut

5g bicarbonate soda

2 fresh bananas (mashed)

Lemon zest (1 lemon)

1 tablespoon lemon essence

Preparation Method

1. Pre heat oven to 180 degrees.
2. Cream the margarine and sugar in a bowl, using a wooden spoon or an electric mixer.
3. Add the whisked eggs and mix in the mashed bananas and walnut and lemon zest.
4. Add in the flour and mix into a smooth batter.
5. Grease a baking tin with some margarine using a pastry brush.
6. Dust the greased tin with some flour to remove excess fat.
7. Pour the batter into the greased tin.
8. Bake in a pre-heated oven at 180 degrees for 40 minutes.
9. Cool and decorate with topping, garnish with lemon zest.

Cakes

Topping

115g butter or margarine

500g icing sugar

Grated lemon zest (1 lemon)

Lemon juice (1 lemon)

Preparation method
1. Mix butter and icing sugar in a bowl, beat until fluffy.
2. Add the lemon juice and zest and mix in.
3. Spread onto the cake.

Banana & Coconut Cake

Ingredients

150g self-raising flour

150g margarine

150g caster sugar

150g egg (whisked)

100ml milk

75g fine dried coconut

5g bicarbonate soda

2 fresh bananas (mashed)

1 tablespoon coconut essence

Cakes

Preparation Method

1. Pre heat oven to 180 degrees.
2. Cream the margarine and sugar in a bowl, using a wooden spoon or an electric mixer.
3. Add the whisked eggs and mix in the mashed bananas and coconut.
4. Add in the flour and mix into a smooth batter.
5. Grease a baking tin with some margarine using a pastry brush.
6. Dust the greased tins with some flour to remove excess fat.
7. Pour the cake batter into the greased baking tin.
8. Bake in a pre-heated oven at 180 degrees for 25 minutes.
9. Cool and decorate with topping.

Topping

25g butter or margarine

10g clear honey

150g fine dried coconut

Preparation method

1. Melt butter and honey in a saucepan.
2. Add the coconut and cook on gentle heat until brown.

Cakes

Fruit cake

Ingredients

250g self-raising flour

200g margarine

200g brown sugar

200g egg

500g mixed dried fruits

2 tbsp black treacle

2 tsp mixed spice

50g chopped nuts (almond)

Preparation Method

1. Pre heat oven to 140 degrees.
2. Place all ingredients in a bowl except fruits and nuts.
3. Mix the ingredients to a paste using a wooden spoon or an electric mixer.
4. Then add the fruits and nuts and stir in.
5. Grease a baking tin with some margarine using a pastry brush.
6. Dust the greased tins with some flour to remove excess fat.
7. Pour the cake mixture into the greased baking tin.
8. Pre heat oven and bake at 140 degrees for 3 hours.
9. Cool and wrap in grease proof paper.
10. Store the cake in an airtight container.
11. Add brandy or whisky every week to increase flavour.
12. Decorate for wedding or parties.

Cakes

Chocolate Sponge Cake

Ingredients

150g self-raising flour

150g butter/margarine

150g caster sugar

150g eggs (whisked)

100g plain chocolate or cocoa powder

Preparation Method

1. Pre heat oven to 180 degrees.
2. Mix the margarine and sugar in a bowl, using a spoon or a mixer until creamy.
3. Add the whisked egg and mix on low speed.
4. Add the flour with the cocoa powder or melted plain chocolate.
5. Mix the cake batter for about 5 minutes.
6. Grease a baking tin with some margarine using a pastry brush.
7. Dust the greased tin with some flour to remove excess fat.
8. Pour the cake batter into the prepared tin.
9. Bake for 40 minutes or until the top is firm to touch.

Cakes

Queen Cupcakes

Ingredients

175g self-raising flour

125g margarine

125g caster sugar

100g eggs (whisked)

20ml milk

Preparation Method

1. Pre heat oven to 170 degrees.
2. Mix the margarine and sugar, using a spoon or an electric mixer.
3. Add the whisked egg and milk gradually.
4. Add the flour and mix for about 5 minutes.
5. Pour into a greased mini cake tins or paper cases.
6. Bake in a pre-heated oven for 15 minutes at 170 degrees.
7. Cool and serve or decorate for party.

Cakes

Muffins

Ingredients

200g self-raising flour

100 margarine (vegetable oil can be used)

130g caster sugar

100g eggs (whisked)

20ml milk

5g nutmeg

10ml vanilla

Preparation Method

1. Pre heat oven to 170 degrees.
2. Mix the egg and sugar in a bowl, using a spoon or an electric mixer.
3. Add the flour and nutmeg and mix into a smooth batter.
4. Melt the margarine in a microwave and add into the mix.
5. Add the milk and vanilla.
6. Mix the cake batter for about 5 minutes.
7. Pour into a greased muffin cake tins or paper muffin cases.
8. Bake in a pre-heated oven for 15 minutes at 170 degrees.
9. Cool and serve or decorate for party.

Cakes

Carrot Cake

Ingredients

175 self raising flour

150ml eggs (3 eggs)

175g caster sugar

150 vegetable oil

5g bicarbonate soda

5g baking powder

10g cinnamon

1 tablespoon vanilla essence

275g carrot (grated)

Rind of orange (1 orange)

40g walnut or hazelnut

Preparation Method

1. Pre heat oven to 180 degrees.
2. Mix egg, sugar, vegetable oil, vanilla in a bowl.
3. Mix flour, bicarbonate soda, baking powder & cinnamon.
4. Add egg mixture into flour mixture and mix into smooth batter.
5. Add the carrot, rind of orange and walnut or hazelnut. Grease a baking tins with some margarine using a pastry brush.
6. Dust the greased tin with some flour to remove excess fat.
7. Pour the cake batter into the greased cake tin.
8. Bake at 180 degrees for 40 minutes.
9. Cool on a cooling wire.

Cakes

Topping

125g cream cheese

50g butter

1 table spoon vanilla essence

100g icing sugar

40g nibbled nuts

Preparation method

1. Mix all ingredient except the nuts until fluffy in a bowl using a whisk.
2. Firm up in fridge for 30 minutes and spread onto cake.
3. Sprinkle nuts onto top of decorated cake.

Desserts

Savoury Scones

225g self raising flour

2.5g cayenne pepper

2.5g salt

50g butter

50ml egg (1 egg)

125ml milk

Preparation method

1. Pre heat oven to 180 degrees.
2. Place all ingredients in a mixing bowl and mix into a dough
3. Knead and roll the dough into ½ inch thickness.
4. Cut the dough into round discs using a cookie cutter
5. Place onto a paper lined baking tray and brush the top with milk
6. Bake in preheated oven at 180 degrees for 15 minutes or until golden brown.
7. Cool and serve

Desserts

Pancake

Ingredients

50g butter/margarine

50g sugar

50g egg

50g flour

50g milk

10ml vegetable oil for frying

Filling

Jam

Sugar

Preparation Method

1. Mix all the main ingredients in a bowl, using a wooden spoon.
2. Heat a saucepan with a little oil.
3. Pour enough batter to cover the base of the pan and cook.
4. Flip the pancake to the other side and fry till golden brown.
5. Place on a plate and add the jam and sugar.
6. Roll up the pancake or fold into four.
7. Ready to serve.

Desserts

Coconut Candy

Ingredients

100g grated coconut

30g granulated sugar or icing sugar

20ml coconut milk or water (optional)

Preparation Method

1. Crack open one large fresh coconut (you may save the milk).
2. Remove the coconut from the shell using a sharp knife.
3. Wash and grate the coconut into a thick bottomed pan.
4. Add the coconut milk (optional)
5. Add the sugar and cook on low heat until golden brown.
6. Cool and roll up into ball shapes.
7. For dried coconut, place stir fried coconut onto baking tray and bake in pre-heated oven at 150 degrees for 10 minutes.
8. Cool, serve or package.

Desserts

Coconut Macaroons

Ingredients

150g fine designated coconut

250g granulated sugar

25g ground rice

100ml egg white

30g plain chocolate (melted for topping) optional

20g dried cherry (for decoration) optional

Preparation Method

1. Pre heat oven to 170 degrees.
2. Place all **ingredients** into a saucepan and heat to 45 degrees on low heat.
3. Place into a piping bag.
4. Pipe onto silicone lined baking trays.
5. Place half cherry on each macaroons to decorate. (Optional)
6. Bake at 170 degrees for 15 minutes.
7. Cool and decorate with spun melted chocolate.

Fresh Fruits and Nuts

Mango

Ingredients

Ripe mango

Preparation Method

1. Peel the mango and cut into small bite size cubes.
2. Place in a bowl.
3. Chill and serve.

Pineapple

Ingredients

Pineapple

Preparation Method

1. Place the pineapple on a clean chopping board.
2. Cut off the top and bottom parts of the pineapple, using a sharp knife.
3. Stand the pineapple upright and cut into four, slicing from the top to the bottom.
4. Place the slices flat on the chopping board, and slice off the fruit from the skin.
5. Slice the fruit into bite sizes and place into a bowl.
6. Chill and serve.

Fresh Fruits and Nuts

Cashew fruit

Ingredients

Cashew fruit

Preparation Method

1. Wash the cashew and serve on a plate.

Watermelon

Ingredients

Watermelon

Preparation Method

1. Place the watermelon on a chopping board.
2. Remove the outer skin and the seeds.
3. Cut into slices or bite sizes.
4. Serve chilled.

Guava

Ingredients

Guava fruit

Preparation Method

1. Wash and serve.

Fresh Fruits and Nuts

Pawpaw (Papaya)

Ingredients

Pawpaw (ripe)

Preparation Method

2. Place the pawpaw on a chopping board
3. Cut off top and bottom parts using a sharp knife.
4. Slice into four from top to bottom.
5. Place the pawpaw slices flat on the board and slice the fruit part from the outer skin.
6. Slice the peeled pawpaw into bite sizes
7. Chill and serve

Bananas

Ingredients

Bananas

Preparation Method

1. Wash and serve.

Sugar Cane

Ingredients

Sugar cane

Preparation Method

1. Peel off the skin from the sugar cane using a sharp knife.
2. Slice the sugar cane into bite sizes.
3. Ready to serve

Fresh Fruits and Nuts

Garden Egg

Ingredients

2 small garden eggs

Preparation Method

1. Wash and serve.

Agbalumo (White Star Apple)

Ingredients

Agbalumo

Preparation Method

1. Wash and serve

Kola nut

Ingredients

Kola nut

Preparation Method

1. Wash and serve.
2. Salt or peanut butter may be provided for dipping.

Orogbo (Bitter Kola)

Ingredients

Orogbo

Preparation Method

1. Wash and serve.

Fresh Fruits and Nuts

Oranges

Ingredients

Orange

Preparation Method
1. Wash and peel off the skin using a knife.
2. Cut into half, place onto a clean plate.
3. Serve

Coconut

Ingredients

Coconut

Preparation method
1. Crack the coconut using a sharp knife or hammer (you may collect the water from the coconut and use as coconut drink).
2. Break open the cracked coconut and cut into pieces.
3. Remove the fruit from the shell using a sharp knife.
4. Cut the fruit into bite sizes and serve.

Drinks

Chapman cocktail

Ingredients

1.5ml Fanta orange

1.5ml bitter lemon

500ml Ribena juice

2 tbsp aromatic bitters

Ice cubes (optional)

2 lemons (sliced)

Preparation Method
1. Pour all the drinks into a jug.
2. Add the aromatic bitters to flavour.
3. Chill or serve with ice cube and lemon slices.

Mango Juice

Ingredients

2 mangoes

Preparation Method
1. Peel and dice the mangoes.
2. Pass through a juicer.
3. Stir, chill and serve garnished with pineapple slices.

Drinks

Pineapple Drink

Ingredients

1 pineapple

Preparation Method

1. Peel the pineapple and pass through a juicer.
2. Serve chilled in a glass.

Orange Juice

Ingredients

3 oranges

Preparation Method

1. Cut the oranges into four, using a knife.
2. Squeeze the juice into a glass cup.
3. Serve chilled.

Drinks

Hot Honey and Lemon Drink

Ingredients

1 lemons

1tbsp honey

300ml hot water

Preparation Method
1. Squeeze lemons into a mug.
2. Boil water in a kettle.
3. Pour into mug.
4. Add honey, stir and serve.

Hot Beverage

Ingredients

2 tsp chocolate powder

300 ml water

20 ml milk (optional)

1 tsp sugar (optional)

Preparation Method
1. Boil the water in a kettle.
2. Pour into a mug.
3. Add the chocolate powder, sugar and milk.
4. Stir and serve.

How to

How to peel yam

Ingredients

Yam tuber

Preparation Method
1. Place the yam on a chopping board or work table.
2. Using a sharp knife cut into slices.
3. Peel the skin off the yam slices.
4. Wash and cook or freeze for later use.

How to peel plantain

Ingredients

Plantain

Processing Method
1. Cut off the top and tail part of the plantain, using a knife.
2. Slit the plantain across the length, using a knife.
3. Place a fingertip in the slit and peel off the skin.
4. Dice or slice to desired shape and sizes.

For green plantain

Drop the plantain in hot water for 1 second to soften skin and follow the above procedure

How To

How to peel beans

Ingredients

Brown beans or white black eyed beans

Processing Method 1
1. Soak the beans in water for at least 1-2 hours.
2. Rub with palm of hands till skins come off.
3. Wash the skin off and use or freeze for later use.

Method 2
1. Soak beans in water for 1 hour.
2. Place the beans in a blender and add water.
3. Turn the blender on and off at quick intervals of about 1 second.
4. Repeat the process, until all the skin is separated from the beans.
5. Wash off the skin and use or freeze for later use.

How to

How to parboil stew for freezer

Ingredients

1.2kg tinned tomatoes (fresh may be used)

2 large red paprika peppers

4 chilli or scotch bonnet pepper

1 large onion

100ml vegetable oil

Processing Method

1. Blend the tomatoes, peppers and onions in a blender.
2. Heat the vegetable oil in a saucepan and pour in the blended tomatoes.
3. Cook for 40mins.
4. Cool, package and freeze for later use.

How to process Egusi seed for cooking

Ingredients

Egusi seed

Preparation Method

1. Grind the whole egusi seeds in a grinder.
2. Package in a plastic bag for later use.
3. To use in cooking, moisten the ground egusi with a little water.
4. Add to vegetable stew to prepare egusi soup.
5. Processing Method 2 (freshly ground)
6. Blend the whole egusi with water to a thick paste.
7. Add to vegetable stew.

How To

How to process okra for cooking

Ingredients

Okra

Processing Method 1
1. Slice the okra into big chunks, using a knife.
2. Place the sliced okra into a blender.
3. Add a little water and roughly blend.

Processing Method 2
Grate the okra on a chopping board using a vegetable grater.

Preparation Method 3
1. Cut the okra into 6 narrow slices, using a knife.
2. Chop the slices into tiny bits using a knife.
3. Add a little water and whisk.
4. Use in okra stew.

How to Prepare Fish

Smoked Fish

Ingredients

Smoked fish

Salt

Processing Method

1. Place the smoked fish in a bowl and add hot water and salt.
2. Soak for 30 minutes, clean the fish and use.

Stock Fish (panla)

Ingredients

Stock fish

Salt

Processing Method

1. Place the stock fish in a bowl and add hot water and salt.
2. Soak overnight, place in a saucepan of water and cook for 1 hour or until soft.
3. Clean the fish, remove any bones and use.

How to clean snails

Ingredients

Snail

Lemon or lime

Alum

Salt

How To

Processing Method
1. Crack the snail and remove the shells.
2. Rub with lime and alum and wash with water.
3. Repeat the process until the snail is sharp to touch.
4. Check the snail is sharp to touch with no slimy feel.
5. Rinse with salt and cook or freeze for later use.

How to fold traditional leaves in cooking moimoi

Materials

Fresh leaves (Ewe known as thaumatococcus danielli leaves)

Moimoi batter (freshly ground soaked beans, pepper, onions, oil and salt)

Processing Method
1. Wash and dry the leaves, Pick one by the stalk and fold into a cone shape.
2. Fold the tail end backwards and hold firmly.
3. Fill the folded cone shaped leaf with moimoi batter to ¾ full.
4. It is important not to over fill, so as to allow room for expansion when cooking and also room to fold the filled leaf over to seal.
5. Fold the top of the leaf to the back to seal and place into a steamer or saucepan of water.
6. Ensure the bottom of the saucepan is raised up with a wire to prevent water getting into the moimoi.
7. Cook for 1 hour, adding a little water during the cooking to avoid the moimoi burning.

How To

How to process gari

Ingredients

Cassava tubers

Processing Method

1. Peel and grate the cassava, place into a sack.
2. Place the sack of grated cassava between two heavy wooden slabs to drain off all the water.
3. Leave to ferment for 3 to 7 days depending on your desired taste.
4. Sieve the cassava to remove the large particles.
5. Roast the cassava in a large wok, stir continuously to prevent the gari burning.
6. Cool and package for later use.

Lafun

Ingredients

Cassava

Processing Method

1. Peel the cassava and soak for 3 days.
2. Mash the soaked cassava, spread out to dry out all the water.
3. Grind to a fine flour, package later use.

How To

How to decorate a cake

Ingredients

Cake
Ready roll on icing
Food colouring
Icing sugar
Jam or butter cream
Egg (white part only)

Processing Method

1. Prepare the cake surface, trim and ensure you have a smooth surface.
2. Coat the top and sides of the cake with jam or butter cream.
3. Roll out the ready roll on icing on icing sugared table.
4. Lift gently with a rolling pin and place carefully onto the cake.
5. Smooth onto the cake top and sides with palm of the hand.
6. Trim off the excess icing at the edges of cake. Set the cake aside.
7. Mix the icing sugar and egg white until it is stiff using a spoon or electric whisk.
8. Add the food colouring and place into a plastic bag with a piping tube.
9. Push the icing onto the cake, both top and bottom edges.
10. Tie a ribbon around the sides for touch of beauty.
11. Place in a cardboard cake box for safe storage and transportation

How To

Tips for decorating queen/ fairy cakes

Ingredients

100g icing sugar

1tbsp cold water

Food colouring

Decorating sugar or coloured sweets

Processing Method
1. Mix the icing sugar and water to a stiff paste.
2. Spread onto the top of the cupcakes with a knife.
3. Place sweets or decorating sugar to desired effects.

How to select menu while feeling poorly or sick

A good appetite for food usually wanes with illness. A few menu selections will help you back to recovery.

Water: Water is good for hydrating the body while appetite is low.

Fresh fruits: Rich in vitamins and can help replenish vitality.

Hot beverage: Chocolate drinks help relax and aid good sleep.

Honey and lemon: This can be prepared hot, it is good for soothing a sore throat.

Mild chilli fish or assorted meat pepper soup: Pepper soup helps clear the tongue and helps the palate recover.

How To

Pap (Ogi): African porridge is light and gentle on the stomach. Serve with plenty of fresh or condensed milk.

Ewedu and amala: This dish is lighter than most heavy meals. It is a good way of introducing solid meals to people recovering from illness.

Suya Meat: This is a savoury delicacy, it has chilli pepper and it helps clear the bitter taste off the tongue.

How to choose a menu for home cooking

Every mother will be familiar with the question of "What is for dinner?" from family members.

It is advisable to select a range of food types. Ensure selection is from a mixture of protein, carbohydrate and fat based meals such as beans and meat dishes, bread, yam and heavy meals to make up a balanced diet.

Lighter meals are usually best for morning meals. A food cooking rota may be drawn up for easy family cooking.

The secret is to do weekly bulk cooking and freeze for later use.

Peeled beans and fried meat can also be prepared and kept frozen for quick meals during the week.

Week 1

Days	Breakfast	Lunch	Dinner
Monday	Boiled yam and egg stew	Fried plantain and stew	Amala and vegetables
Tuesday	Toast and boiled egg	Moimoi and gari	Boiled rice and
Wednesday	Cereal, toast and butter	Ground rice and okra stew	Fried rice and fried fish
Thursday	Boiled yam and garden egg stew	Rice and beans with stew	Pounded yam and vegetable stew
Friday	Boiled plantain and stew	Eba and ogbono stew	Moimoi and eko
Saturday	Akara and pap	Amala and ewedu stew	Beans and sweetcorn
Sunday	Moimoi and pap	Traditional pounded yam with egusi stew	Jollof rice and beef with plantain

Week 2

Days	Breakfast	Lunch	Dinner
Monday	Boiled yam and egg stew	Boiled rice and stew	Semovita and vegetable stew
Tuesday	Beans and loaf bread	Fufu and vegetable	Rice and beans with stew
Wednesday	Cereal, toast and butter	Fried rice, salad and meat	Roast chicken with salad and yam chips
Thursday	Boiled potatoes and stew	Beans and yam	Eba and okra stew
Friday	Loaf bread and egg and sardine stew	Moimoi and gari	Boiled rice and stew
Saturday	Akara and pap	Amala and ewedu stew	Beans and sweetcorn
Sunday	Toast, bacon and egg	Yam porridge	Semovita and vegetable stew

Week 3

Days	Breakfast	Lunch	Dinner
Monday	Akara and pap	Yam chips and egg	Amala and vegetables
Tuesday	Moimoi and pap	Jollof rice with plantain	Pounded yam and vegetable stew
Wednesday	Boiled yam with stew	Fufu and vegetable stew	Fried rice and fried fish
Thursday	Cereal, toast and butter	Rice and beans with stew	Moimoi and eko
Friday	Beans with loaf bread	Eba and ogbono stew	Coconut rice with stew
Saturday	Cereal, toast and butter	Yam porridge with stew	Amala with vegetable stew
Sunday	Toast, bacon and egg	Traditional pounded yam with egusi stew	Jollof rice and beef with plantain

Week 4

Days	Breakfast	Lunch	Dinner
Monday	Cereal and toast	Boiled rice and stew	Amala and vegetable
Tuesday	Moimoi and pap	Jollof rice and chicken	Eba and vegetable stew
Wednesday	Boiled yam and plantain with stew	Amala and vegetable stew	Fried rice and fried fish
Thursday	Boiled potatoes and stew	Beans and gari	Semovita and vegetable stew
Friday	Loaf bread and beans	Eba and ogbono stew	Moimoi and eko
Saturday	Akara and pap	Yam porridge and stew	Rice & Beans with stew
Sunday	Cereal, toast and egg	Roast chicken, salad and chips	coconut rice with stew

Healthy Eating

Another question I get asked from friends and family is: what food do I eat to lose weight? I believe you are what you eat, and the secret to successful eating is a balanced diet. Select a diet rich in vegetables, fruits, water, protein, a bit of fat and high in fibre.

Below are some ideas of food to eat or avoid. Also an idea of what to put in that shopping trolley. (Please note the writer lives in London UK and the suggested items are food readily available in the UK).

<u>Healthy weight watching ideas</u>

Breakfast
- Oat
- Wheat cereal
- Wholemeal bread
- Egg
- Fruits
- Green tea
- Avoid processed meat (sausages, bacon, ham etc.)
- Avoid concentrated fruit juices (only freshly juiced fruits)
- Healthy yoghurt

Lunch
- Homemade sandwich
- Fruits
- Vegetable juice (carrot, beetroot, kale)
- Water with 1 lemon squeezed in
- Beans
- Home cooked vegetable soups

Dinner
- Roast chicken (fresh not frozen) with boiled baby potatoes and steamed vegetables e.g. broccoli, cauliflower and carrots.
- Grilled fish with stir fried quinoa or couscous with lots of vegetables.

- Spinach (efo riro) with amala (avoid too much of carbohydrate).
- Brown Rice (eat with lots of vegetables).
- Beef, roast potatoes and steamed vegetables.

Shopping list
- Oat cereal
- Shredded wheat
- Butter (avoid margarine)
- Eggs
- Almond milk
- Skimmed milk
- Fish
- Chicken
- Beef
- Vegetables
- Spinach
- Kale
- Carrots
- Broccoli
- Beetroot
- Brussel sprouts
- Beans (Nigerian)
- Yam
- Plantain
- Fresh herbs e.g. parsley
- Baby potatoes
- Red onions
- Garlic
- Ginger
- Cauliflower
- Brussel sprout
- Potatoes
- Birds eye chilli pepper
- Large red pepper
- Tomatoes

Healthy Eating

- Quinoa/Couscous
- Brown rice
- Lemon and limes
- Green tea
- Apples
- Bananas
- Mangoes
- Oranges
- Blueberries
- Grapes
- Olive oil or sunflower oil for cooking
- Yoghurt
- Seaweed
- Prawns
- Nuts

Food to Avoid

- Sugar
- Concentrated fruit juice
- Salt (6g per day)
- Processed and freezer food (cook meals from scratch and freeze)
- Burgers, pizzas, chips, coffees
- Too much carbohydrate e.g. bread, rice etc.
- Puddings and desserts e g cakes, ice cream, chocolates, sweets, biscuits etc. (except for treat)

Tips

Add fresh ginger, fresh chillies, fresh herbs and red onion into cooking, they quicken metabolism.

Exercise Daily (at least 20 minutes)

- Skipping
- Cross trainer
- Treadmill
- Running
- Walking

Drink

- Lots of water at least 6- 8 glasses per day
- Green tea (cleanses the system)
- Avoid alcohol
- Avoid coffee
- Avoid hot chocolate or cocoa drink
- Lemon squeezed into hot or cold water
- Ginger tea
- Lemon tea

Food to Love

Fruits and vegetables - at least five portions per day.

Eating Habits

The simple guide to eating is to be disciplined. Let nature determine your eating habits, eat only when you are hungry. Avoid cravings, snacks and comfort eating.

Healthy Eating Food Chart

Exercise daily

Drink at least 6 -8 glasses of water per day

Eat at least 5-7 servings of fruit and vegetables per day

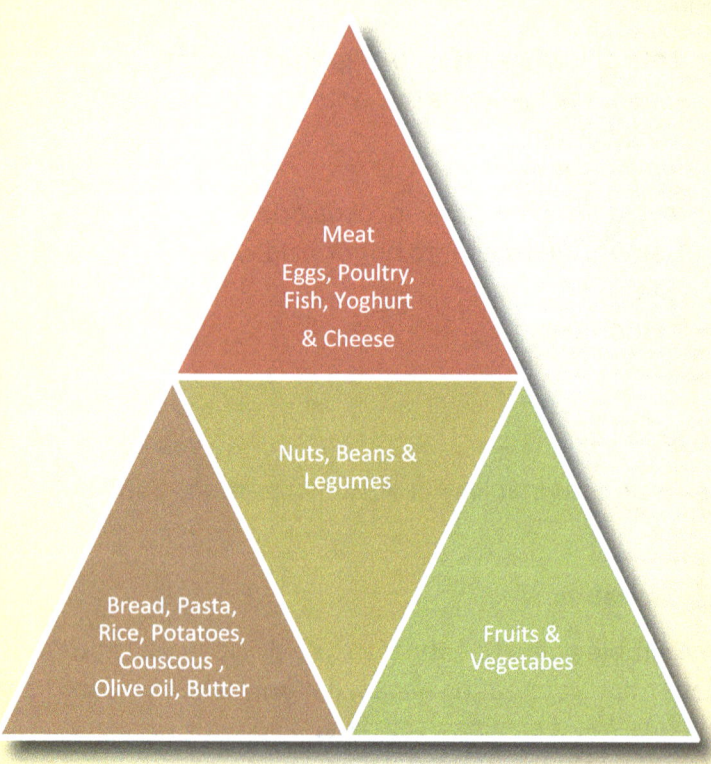

Eat more food from the bottom of the Pyramid and less from the top

How to plan Weddings and Parties

A wedding proposal comes with great excitement. To have a successful wedding party, good planning is essential. It is advisable to allow plenty of time for the planning, usually 3 to 12 months. There will be four great decisions and questions to answer.

- When is the day?
- Where will it be held?
- How much will it cost?
- What theme will it be?

Careful consideration of the above questions will ensure a successful event.

How to decide the date

Call a meeting with the immediate family members and the parents to choose a date.

Choose a date that is convenient for both family members.

Send out emails to loved ones to check if response is good for attendance.

How to choose a venue

- Call the venues of your choice around the location desired.
- Ask how many guests the venue can hold.
- What facilities such as kitchen, toilets and parking spaces does it have?
- What equipment is included in package?
- Do they permit use of outside caterers?
- Is there an in-house PA system?
- Are there tables and chairs?
- Are there adequate quantities of tables and chairs?

How to plan Weddings and Parties

- Do the tables and chairs match your seating plan and shapes?
- Does the venue need extra decoration?
- Will there be disabled facilities?
- Is there adequate ventilation and heating?
- Are there staff to oversee things on the day?
- Is there spare room for the host and bride changing time?
- Is there water, soap and tissue for toilets?
- Is cleaning in the package and to what extent.
- Is rubbish removal in the package?
- Is furniture clearing in the package?
- How much will it cost and how is payment taken?
- What are the terms and conditions?

How to plan African attire (Aso Ebi)
- Decide whether African costume will be required.
- Choose fabric with colours to match wedding theme colours.
- Make a list of family members and friends for fabrics.
- Shop around African fabric shops and select one within budget.
- Ask family and friends to buy from a person in charge.
- Book tailors for sewing the materials (allow time at least three months).

How to decorate
- Consider professional decorators.
- What table decoration (fresh flowers, candles or balloons)?
- Do you want chair covers?
- What colour and material of table cover and napkins?

How to plan Weddings and Parties

- What is the seating arrangement?
- Is there seating cards for arranged seats?
- Are there name boards for arranged seats?
- Has invitation being done as strictly by invitation?
- Do you require a top table?
- What decoration do you prefer for top table?
- Are there adequate favours and gifts?
- Is there a cake table and table cloth?
- What decoration do you prefer for the cake table?
- Is there a cake knife and does it need decoration?
- Do you require a stage for a live band?
- Does the venue provide stage and dance floor?

How to choose a caterer
- Ask for referrals and recommendation.
- Choose a reputable caterer.
- Request a menu or prepare your own.
- Have a tasting session to help decide for taste.
- Decide the service style (buffet or seated).
- Have a consultation session with the caterer.
- Are they providing drinks?
- What is the cost?
- What equipment do they supply (crockery, glasses)?
- Do they supply professional waiting staff?
- What is their food presentation like?
- Would they cook on or off site?

How to plan Weddings and Parties

- How will food be transported?
- Is there sufficient cooking time and enough time to transport to venue?
- What is the cleaning and rubbish removal arrangement?
- How many hours will they work?
- How is payment taken?
- Is there a need for a contract?
- Do they have a professional kitchen they work from?
- Are they experienced in the cuisine you are choosing?
- Do they have equipment or will they hire?
- Do their choice of crockery and cutlery meet your standard?
- Do they understand your vision for the day?
- Can they meet your standard of how you want things done?

How to choose staff for the day
- Family service may be used but professional staff is best.
- Check staff are trained and with adequate uniform.
- Staffs should be briefed and specific tasks assigned to staff.
- Staff must understand food service timing, menus and drinks.
- Staff have late night transportation arranged.
- Efficient bar staff booked.
- Staff are cheerful and polite.
- Are there adequate numbers of staff to guests? (Minimum one staff to 30 guests.)
- Are they wearing comfortable shoes?
- How much will they cost?

How to plan Weddings and Parties

How to plan for after event clearing
- Check venue's clearing and cleaning arrangement plan.
- Check caterer's responsibility for kitchen cleaning.
- Have professional cleaners if needed.
- Have family members to remove left over drinks and gifts.
- Ensure decorators and hire companies are booked for equipment collection.
- Ensure accommodation is booked for host or far away guests if required.
- Is there recycling provision for drink bottles and cans?
- In what condition must the venue be returned to the manager?

How to choose drink for weddings
Which wine?
- Most West African meals will go well with any white or red wine. The usual custom is to place a bottle each of red wine (room temperature) and chilled white wine on each table. Waiters will top up from the bar as required.

Juice
- Fruit juices of any flavour go well with African meals. This may be placed directly onto tables or in a jug with or without ice cubes.
- Allow one 1.5ltr per four guests

Mineral water
- Still or sparkling distilled water should be provided both at bar and dining tables.
- Allow 1.5ltr bottle per four guests or 330ml bottle per guest.

Fizzy drinks
- Bottled or canned drinks may be served from the bar.

How to plan Weddings and Parties

Malt

Malt drink is very popular at Nigerian parties, especially with elderly guests.

Alcohol

Canned beers and alcohol should be served from a bar supervised by licensed person.

Tips: Allow extra glasses at the bar and for reception cocktail.

How to make a temporary bar

Most venues will have a bar but where there is none follow the method below:

Method
- Select a trestle or any solid rectangular or square table.
- Cover with a linen cloth.
- Chill the drink with ice and keep under the table if a fridge is not provided.
- Place ice bucket and tongs on the table.
- Place jugs of juice and other drinks on the table.
- Arrange a few glasses in triangle and stack up to a pyramid shape.
- The bar is ready to use.

How to plan Weddings and Parties

Drink shopping quantity guide

It is good etiquette for host to buy plenty of drink. However, it is cost effective to plan drink quantities to avoid wastage. See guide table below:

Table 1

Drink Type	Per	Guest No.
Wine	750ml bottle	Four guests
Juice	1.5ltr box	Four guests
Mineral water	1.5ltr bottle	Four guests
Malt	330ml bottle	One guest
Canned drink	330ml can	One guest
Bottled fizzy drink	1.5ltr bottle	Four guests

How to plan Weddings and Parties

How to select menu for wedding or fine dining parties

Every dining experience has an average of one to five course meals.

Cocktail Reception : canapés or snacks such samosa, spring rolls, chin chin, stick meat with a cocktail drink such as chapman or sparkling wine or juice make a good food and drink menu.

First Course: Starter can be fruit kebab, oriental spring rolls on lettuce, pepper soup with bread roll and butter. These are good first course menu suggestions.

Second Course: Main course can have a range of food from the light meal selection of this book. Rice dishes such as jollof rice and meat in pepper garnishing are great examples.

Third Course: For dessert menu, selection can be a range of cakes or fruit salads. Wedding cake may also be used for dessert menu.

Afters: Cheese board, fresh fruit, crisps, mint chocolates or tea and coffee may be offered.

Wedding Menu Ideas

MENU A

Starter
Assorted Meat Pepper Soup
Fish Pepper soup
Bread Roll & Butter

Main Course
Jollof Rice
Stir Fried Noodles
Yam Porridge & Stew
Plain Rice & Ayamase Stew
Gizzard and Plantain
Fried Beef in Pepper Garnish
Fried Chicken in Pepper Garnish
Fried Fish in Pepper Garnish
Mixed Leaf Salad

Dessert
Strawberry Cheesecake
Exotic fruit salad

Wedding Menu Ideas

Menu B

Starter
Spring Rolls

Samosa

King Prawns

Main Course
Coleslaw

Special Fried Rice

Jollof Rice

Grilled Fish with Peppers & Onions

Fried Beef Pieces in Pepper & Onions

Barbecue Chicken

Plantain

Moi moi

Dessert
Mini Profiterole Towers

Exotic Fruit Salad

Wedding Menu Ideas

MENU C

Starter

Chin Chin

Meat Pies

Bun/Puff Puff

Main Course

Curry Goat

Beef in Pepper Garnish

Jollof Rice

Rice & Peas

Fried Plantain

Fried Fish with Mixed Peppers

Coleslaw

Yam Porridge & Stew

Dessert

Fresh Fruit

Carrot Cake with Cream

Wedding Menu Ideas

MENU D

Starter

Stick Meat with Mixed Pepper

Assorted Meat Pepper Soup

Bread Roll & Butter

Main Course

Stir Fried Noodles

Beans & Stew

Jollof Rice

Yam porridge & Stew

Fried Fish in Pepper

Fried Beef in Pepper

Fried Chicken in Pepper

Fresh Salad

Fried Plantain

Dessert

Apple Pies & Custard

Selection of tarts

Wedding Menu Ideas

MENU E

Starter
Plantain and Gizzard Kebab

King Prawn

Main Course
Jollof Rice

Rice & Peas

Curry Goat

Grilled Fish with Mixed Peppers

Barbecue Chicken

Fried Plantain

Steamed Vegetables

New Potatoes

Dessert
Exotic Fruits

Selection of Cheese Cake

Event day final check list

- Is there a guest list?
- Has everyone on the list been sent invitation?
- Is there contingency plan for uninvited guests?
- Are road maps sent with invitations?
- Is equipment booked with plenty of time for delivery and collection?
- Is the caterer allocated packing space and use of kitchen and serving area?
- Is Hire Company booked?
- Are music and entertainers booked with space allocated for them?
- Is there provision for a dance area?
- Is PA system in working order?
- Is floor plan done with spaces for all workers?
- Is top table marked reserved?
- Is decorator and florist booked with plenty of time to get venue ready?
- Are all contractors reputable and reliable suppliers?
- Is there an event coordinator to supervise all contractors and staff?
- Is the cake booked for delivery and cake knife hired?
- What is the weather forecast for the day?
- Are there sufficient drinks for the day?
- Is there adequate transportation for drinks and equipment?
- Is the bride and groom clothes ready and in correct sizes
- Are all suppliers paid and firmly booked?
- Are all furniture and equipment in good order?
- Is there a cake table?
- Can staff get to venue by public transport or is there a need for taxi?

Other types of parties

The list of parties, why and when is endless with Africans. A good organisation and planning ability is critical for successful entertainment. Family and friends can be used to cook, serve and clear away but for peace of mind, professional caterers will be best. Ask friends to recommend as it is best to deal with caterers with good experience and skill, for example Beautiful Foods Ltd.

Theme & Venue for Parties

- Picnic Parties
- Garden Parties
- Hall Parties
- Church Thanksgiving
- Barbecue
- Marquee and canopies
- Banqueting Parties
- Beach Parties
- Boat Parties
- Children's Parties
- Street Parties
- Cruise Parties
- Hotel Parties
- Office Parties
- Costume Parties
- Park parties

Picnic Menu Ideas

- Meat pie
- Sausage roll
- Fish rolls
- Puff puff
- Plantain crisps
- Cake
- Buns
- Scotch egg
- Chin Chin
- Suya meat
- Jollof rice
- Fresh fruits & Vegetable

Photo gallery

Starter, Main Dish & Dessert

Starter showing oriental spring rolls & sauce

Buffet (Jollof, Rice, Fried Rice & Assorted Meat)

Tabitha's Chin Chin

Tabitha's Chin Chin

Top table decoration

Table setting & Decoration

Wedding

Glossary

- **Accompaniment:** These are meals that complement the main dish. In Africa meals meat, fish, chicken are used as accompaniment. If you have jollof rice and beef, jollof rice will be the main course and the beef just an accompaniment, this goes the other way round with English dining where the rice will be the side dish and the beef will be the main course.
- **Akara:** This is a cake made from beans and served at breakfast.
- **Ayamase:** This is a stew made from green peppers and flavoured with iru.
- **Beans:** The black-eyed beans or brown beans are legumes. They are sub species of the cowpea.
- **Egg wash:** This is beaten egg whisked with a little water or milk to give baked pastry a gloss finish.
- **Egusi:** Melon seeds used in cooking as a vegetable.
- **Ewedu:** This is a flowering plant used as vegetable in stew.
- **Gari:** Gari is made from fermented cassava tuber.
- **Heavy meal:** Heavy meals are usually made from yam, cassava or plantain. They are cooked in hot water into a dough and served with stews.
- **Iru:** This is locust beans used in flavouring stew.
- **Isapa:** This is the flower from hibiscus plant used in cooking soup or drinks.
- **Kola nut:** This is the fruit of Kola tree, it contains caffeine.
- **Moimoi:** This is a pudding made from beans.
- **Ofada:** Local rice grown in Nigeria.

- **Okra:** This is a flowering plant in the mallow family. The green seed pod is used for cooking.
- **Palm oil:** This is edible oil derived from the fruit of oil palm.
- **Pap:** This is corn meal cooked to make porridge and served as breakfast meal.
- **Plantain:** This is the fruit produced by herbaceous plant. It is similar to banana but it's used in cooking.
- **Scotch bonnet:** This is variety of pepper similar to chilli. It is also known as Cayenne pepper.
- **Snail:** These are slug-like animals made into spicy meat delicacy.
- **Suya:** This is a special spice made with mixture of ground peppers with ground peanut.
- **Street snack:** Some food items are known as street snacks in Africa. These food items are readily available from open market and road side stalls.
- **Tbsp:** Tablespoon
- **Tsp:** Teaspoon
- **Yam:** Yam is a vegetable cooked to make porridge and served at breakfast.

Index

A
Aadun (ground roasted corn snack), 19
Aayamase Stew, 76
Accompaniments, 84-86
Agbalumo, 125
Akara (Beans cake), 20
Amala, 96
Assorted stick meat, 29-30
Assorted Suya Snack, 16

B
Bananas, 124
Banana & Coconut Cake, 110-111
Banana Sponge Cake, 108
Banana Walnut & Lemon Cake, 109
Banga, 82
Barbecue chicken, 26
Beans, 56-58
Beans and Boiled Yam, 56
Beans and Sweetcorn, 55
Bitter leaf soup, 81
Boiled Corn (Corn on the Cob), 12
Boiled Groundnut, 19
Boiled Plantain, 13
Boiled rice (White Rice), 50-51
Boiled Sweet Potatoes, 61
Boiled yam, 52
Buns, 39
Butter biscuits, 102-103

C
Cakes, 105-117
Carrot Cake, 116-117
Cashew fruit, 123
Chapman cocktail 127
Chin Chin, 24-25
Chocolate chip cookies, 104
Chocolate Sponge Cake, 113
Coconut, 126
Coconut Candy, 120
Coconut Macaroons, 121
Coconut rice, 59
Cocoyam, 64
Coleslaw, 84

D
Desserts, 118-120
Drinks, 127-129
Dry Roasted Peanut, 18

E
Eba, 95
Edikang Ikong, 80
Egg stew, 68
Egusi and Isapa with assorted meat, 71
Egusi with spinach, 70
Event day final check list, 162
Ewedu (Jute or Marlow

leaves), 83
Exercise Daily, 148

F

Fish pepper soup, 44-45
Fish Pie/Roll, 37-38
Fresh fruits and nuts, 122-126
Fried beef in pepper garnishing, 90
Fried chicken in Pepper Garnishing, 88-89
Fried Fish in Pepper Garnishing, 91
Fried plantain, 60
Fried rice, 49-50
Fried Yam chips, 29
Fruit cake, 112
Fruit Skewer, 100-101
Fruit Salad, 99-100
Fufu, 97

G

Garden Egg, 75, 125
Gari (roasted ground cassava), 61
Genoese Cake, 107
Glossary, 170-171
Grilled fish & lemon wedges, 46
Ground rice, 96
Guava 123

H

Health & Safety, 7-9

Healthy Eating 144-148
Healthy weight watch ideas, 144-147
Heavy Meals, 93-98
Home Cooking Menu ideas, 140-143
Hot Beverage, 129
Hot Honey and Lemon Drink, 129
How -To, 130-139
How To...
- choose a caterer, 151
- choose a venue, 149
- choose drink for weddings, 153-155
- choose menu for home cooking, 139-143
- choose staff for the day, 152
- clean snails, 134-135
- decide the date, 149
- decorate, 150
- decorating cakes, 137-138
- fold traditional leaves in cooking moi moi, 135
- make a temporary bar, 154
- make short crust pastry (Sausage Roll recipe) 33
- par boil stew for freezer, 132
- peel beans, 131
- peel plantain, 130
- process Egusi seed for cooking 132
- process okra for cooking 133
- peel yam, 130

- plan African attire (Aso Ebi), 150
- plan Weddings and Parties, 149
- prepare smoked fish 134
- process Egusi seed for cooking, 132
- process gari, 136
- process okra for cooking, 133
- select menu for wedding or fine dining parties, 156
- select menu while feeling poorly or sick, 138

I
Isi ewu (Igbo traditional goat head pepper soup), 43

J
Jollof Rice, 47-48

K
Kola nuts, 125

L
Lafun, 136

M
Madeira cake, 105
Main Meals, 56-64
Mango, 122
Mango Juice, 127
Meat pie (minced meat & potato Patties), 30-32
Menus, 157-161, 140-143

Milk Bread, 65
Mixed vegetable salad, 86
Moimoi, 62-63
Muffins 115

O
Ofada rice (Nigerian local rice), 59
Ogbono, 74
Ojojo (water yam cakes), 21
Okra (plain), 72
Okra in stew, 73
Oranges, 126
Orange Juice, 128
Orogbo, 125
Other African Parties, 163

P
Pancake, 119
Pap (Ogi or akamu), 62
Pawpaw (papaya), 124
Pepper Soup (assorted goat meat), 41-42
Photo gallery, 165-169
Picnic Menu Ideas, 164
Pineapple drink, 128
Plantain Crisps, 22-23
Pounded yam (flour mix), 97
Puff Puff (African doughnut), 40
Pumpkin Stew, 78

R

Roasted Corn (barbecue corn), 12

Roast Peanuts & Popcorn, 18-19

Roasted Plantain (barbecue plantain), 13

Roasted Yam (barbecue yam), 14

S

Salads, 84-85
Sausage Roll, 33-34
Savoury scones, 118
Scotch Egg (savoury), 27-28
Semovita, 98
Shopping list, 145
Snail in Pepper Garnishing, 92
Soup and Starters, 41-45
Sourcing Ingredients 10-11
Spicy gizzard in pepper garnishing, 87
Stews, 66-83
Stock Fish (panla), 134
Street & Finger Snacks, 12-40
Sugar cane, 124
Suya (Beef Kebab), 14-15

T

Theme and Venue for Parties, 163
Tips for decorating queen/ fairy cake, 138
Tomato and lettuce salad, 84

Traditional Pounded Yam, 93-94
Tropical Fruit Salad, 99
Types of Parties, 163

U

Uha soup, 79

V

Vegetable pie, 35-36
Vegetable Stew (Efo Riro), 69
Victoria Sponge Cake, 106

W

Watermelon, 123
Wedding Menu ideas, 157-161

Y

Yam porridge, 53-54

www.ingramcontent.com/pod-product-compliance
Lightning Source LLC
Chambersburg PA
CBHW050638300426
44112CB00012B/1851